What Others Are About Debra Jason and This Book

"When an author claims to teach marketing and writing with heart and not hype, there is a chance that she's setting herself up for disaster . . . but not Debra Jason.

"You will marvel at how she is 100% consistent with that claim in her new book, *Millionaire Marketing on a Shoestring Budget*; but more importantly, she will inspire you to find your own heart (without hype of course!) in whatever you pursue in life.

"Debra sets the bar very high for herself . . . and for all of us. She understands what it truly means to be rich (of which money is only one aspect).

"Her step-by-step approach on how to gain the kind of wealth we desire—financial AND emotional—makes this book a must-read for anyone craving the freedom of entrepreneurship with the ability to express themselves fully in all they do."

— Brian Kurtz
Executive Vice President, Boardroom Inc.
(and Serial Direct Marketer)

"Debra Jason's new book *Millionaire Marketing on a Shoestring Budget* is filled with inspiration combined with step-by-step practical advice on how you can market your business. It has everything from writing effective press releases to social media to powerhouse networking. Each chapter has an exercise for you to complete so you don't just read the words, you put them into action. This is a must-read for anyone who is starting a business on a budget and wants to look like a rock star. Debra has nailed it!"

— Andrea Vahl
Co-author of *Facebook Marketing All-in-One for Dummies*
www.AndreaVahl.com

"Debra Jason's *Millionaire Marketing on a Shoestring Budget* is a practical, revealing and comprehensive guide to gaining exposure for your business without spending the big bucks! If you want to thrive in ANY economy, grab this book now and start putting it into action today!"

— Ken McArthur
Best-Selling Author of *Impact: How to Get Noticed,
Motivate Millions and Make a Difference in a Noisy World*
www.KenMcArthur.com

"Debra is an amazing writer. I read every word in this book and loved it! It is the ultimate resource for anyone who wants to succeed in a big way, but only has a small marketing budget. Debra's brilliant and creative ideas come from her real-life experience in building her own business. Put them to use in marketing your business and your bank account will benefit as a result."

— Patrick Snow
International Best-Selling Author of *Creating Your Own Destiny,
The Affluent Entrepreneur* and *Boy Entrepreneur*
www.PatrickSnow.com

"Debra's book is a fantastic guide not only to marketing on a shoe-string, but also on being in the right frame of mind and attitude to maximize the effectiveness of your marketing. Through simple, 'non-jargon' marketing tips and quick, fun exercises, Debra clearly presents how spending your marketing dollars wisely can lead to huge marketing results. This is a book every entrepreneur and small business owner can benefit from!"

— Kevin Knebl
International Speaker/Author/Trainer/Coach
Co-author of *The Social Media Sales Revolution*
www.KevinKnebl.com

"This extremely practical book is a 'must-have' gem for any small business. Put the tried and true creative marketing strategies into practice, and they can positively impact your bottom line."

— Susan Friedmann, CSP
International Best-Selling Author of
Riches in Niches: How to Make It BIG in a Small Market

"Debra has written a fabulous book that every entrepreneur and small business owner should read. Many marketing books are simply an overview of concepts, but Debra's book is chock-full of easy-to-implement, extremely beneficial tips and techniques to successfully market your business. I found an 'ah-ha' tip in every chapter!"

— Deb Krier, The SociaLight
www.DebKrier.com

"When Debra told me she was going to write this book, I couldn't wait to see it become a reality. Her first-hand experience in building a successful business based on a dream and desire, but without a degree in writing or marketing, allows her to share from a real-world perspective what works and why. Debra's story and success are an inspiration to those of us who are blessed to know her as a friend and colleague, and now you can be inspired, too!"

— Michelle Shaeffer
Girl Blogger Next Door and Co-Founder of
The Ultimate Blog Challenge
www.MichelleShaeffer.com

"Whether you're just getting started or are ready to take your business further, this book reveals the promotional strategies you'll need to develop top of mind awareness. Follow Debra's guidance so that you can enjoy marketing your business, increasing your client base and earning more!"

— Heather Allen, MBA
Author of *Let Your Creativity Work for You*

"Wow! There is a lot of information in this book. *Millionaire Marketing on a Shoestring Budget* is a compelling read. . . . Marketing today is no longer as simple as creating TV or newspaper ads that cost large sums of money—it is about doing a series of things to bring awareness to your brand, many of which you can do for little or no money. Debra Jason doesn't just list a few ideas—she gives you insights and exercises on how to kill it with your marketing without spending a fortune.

"She expands upon the works of others, quoting some true legends and icons of the business world, as well as drawing on the experiences of contemporary entrepreneurs who are creating and implementing the strategies she outlines in this essential book for business owners."

— Greg Jameson
Best-Selling Author of *Amazon's Dirty Little Secrets*
www.WebStoresLtd.com

"The one thing I love about Debra Jason's *Millionaire Marketing on a Shoestring Budget* is that she speaks to you as though you were sitting next to her, like an old friend. Her story is inspirational and heartwarming, especially when she talks about her sweet dog, Ike. She offers exercises that are brilliant and easy to do (one of my favorites is in Chapter 3). This book should be on the desk of every person who wants to learn about marketing as told by the expert, Debra Jason."

— Arlene Krantz
Author of *The Business Within You*

"The truth is, if you want to gain exposure for your business and develop a stream of happy clients, you should start right here with this book."

— Nicole Gabriel
Author of *Finding Your Inner Truth*

"Marketing is a part of everyday life. And Debra Jason is a marketing genius who has taken this broad topic and broken it down into simple, action items that anyone can implement immediately. It's a 'must–read' if you're serious about how to apply practical techniques that will grow your business."

— Lisa Marie Platske
Author of *Connection: The New Currency*
President, Upside Thinking, Inc. and Founder of
the Leadership Success Summit
www.LeadershipSuccessSummit.com

"Success online is, and always will be, based on doing two things well: Adding value to the lives of others with the products or services you offer and getting the word out via promotion.

"It's not enough to publish a great book or create an amazing product/service. It's imperative that you get your message out there to reach the masses who want what you have to offer.

"This is exactly what Debra Jason reveals in *Millionaire Marketing on a Shoestring Budget*. She shares how you can drive traffic in a cost-effective manner, leverage partnerships, maximize your social media marketing efforts *and* a lot more. I highly recommend this book as well as Debra's services."

— Brian G. Johnson
Author of *Trust Funnel*
www.MarketingEasyStreet.com

"In *Millionaire Marketing on a Shoestring Budget*, Debra nails affordable and highly effective marketing tactics. She delivers simple and fun strategies that you can apply to your business right away. As a great companion to my book, I plan to use her concepts with my own clients."

— David Bryant Mitchell
Author of *Building Your Booming Business,*
Professional Keynote Speaker and Business Consultant

"As a marketing professional, I often read books by other 'marketing professionals' and sometimes wonder if they have ever owned their own businesses. In Debra's case, I know that she has operated her own successful business just by reading the insights and strategies she presents in her book.

"She knows what it takes for other entrepreneurs to market their businesses successfully. It's really refreshing to read a book that can absolutely transform any small business if the reader simply follows Debra's advice."

— MJ Jensen
Chief Idea Officer, IdeaMagic visionary marketing & social media
and Founder of Tucson Marketing Professionals

"If you want to travel the road to success and make more money without spending more money, *Millionaire Marketing* shows you how. With more than two decades of experience running her own business, trust Debra as she presents you with a road map that helps you navigate your way!"

— Jim R. Jacobs LCSW
Author of *Driving Lessons for Life: Thoughts on
Navigating Your Road to Personal Growth*

"First impressions will make or break any business, and when it comes to marketing, perception is reality. All the more reason why it is essential to have an expert like Debra behind you. In her book *Millionaire Marketing on a Shoestring Budget*, Debra provides the essential tools to ensure that your business has a leading edge over the competition and that it remains profitable. What a small investment for such great returns. A truly valuable book!"

— Roxana Bowgen
Author of *Agapanthus Rising* and Founder of Volunteers on Call, Inc.

"Who says you can't get blood from a turnip? Debra Jason shows us how to market not through flashy ads and marketing materials, but by making the real-life connections that matter. In the process, hardly a penny need be spent, yet the results can be astounding. Anyone who is selling anything needs to invest in this book. The payoff is well worth the expense."

— Tyler R. Tichelaar, Ph.D.
Award-Winning Author of *The Gothic Wanderer* and *Arthur's Legacy*

"The path to success may be wrought with overwhelming odds and challenges that can stop so many of us from reaching our dreams of entrepreneurship. In Debra Jason's *Millionaire Marketing on a Shoestring Budget*, you will discover how to get your message out there, get noticed and become the financial success you were destined to be without draining your bank account in the process."

— Luis De La Fuente
Author of *Life Lessons From The Lantern*

"Millionaire Marketing on a Shoestring Budget puts it ALL together for the entrepreneur who is passionate about what they do, but unclear about how to market their business. It's an enjoyable read that reveals clear-cut and cost-effective ways to make your business shine, thrive and profit. Dig in and do what Debra Jason tells you—your business will soon be on the fast track to success!"

— Kathleen Swiderski, The Brand Therapist
Red Sky Design & Communications

Millionaire Marketing
on a Shoestring Budget™

How to Attract a Steady Stream
of Happy Clients, Make More Money
and Live Your Dream

Debra Jason

Bethany,

Thanks a million. Now is the
time to live your dream!

Debra

AVIVA
PUBLISHING
New York

Millionaire Marketing on a Shoestring Budget™
How to Attract a Steady Stream of Happy Clients, Make More Money and Live Your Dream

Copyright © 2015 by Debra Jason

www.MillionaireMarketingOnAShoestringBudget.com
www.DebraJason.com
www.WriteDirection.com

ISBN: 978-1-940984-71-1

Library of Congress Control Number: 2014921179

Editor: Tyler Tichelaar
Cover/Interior Book Design: Kathleen Swiderski, Red Sky Design & Communications
Author Photo: Karen Dombrowski-Sobel

Every attempt has been made to identify properly and verify all quotes. This book also includes references to websites, effective at the time this book was written. It is possible that these links may change over time. These references are provided for your convenience to provide further information. Their presence does not signify that Debra Jason endorses the websites. And she has no responsibility for the content of the linked websites referred to herein.

Printed in the United States of America.

Published by Aviva Publishing
Lake Placid, NY
518-523-1320
www.AvivaPubs.com

First edition

2 4 6 8 10

For additional copies visit: www.MillionaireMarketingOnAShoestringBudget.com

Dedication

To my loving parents, Edith and Bernie Jason—the first entrepreneurial role models I had. My mom started her own real estate firm with several of her girlfriends. Dedicated to providing for his family and going above and beyond to serve his clients, my dad ran his own CPA firm for close to forty years.

You are the two people who inspired, supported and loved me through thick and thin. You are always in my heart and with me in spirit. I love and miss you every day and hope you are proud of me.

To my older brother Jack, who currently runs his own business, and my younger brother Steven, who was an entrepreneur at an early age, starting his own car wash business at age eleven. Growing up as the only girl certainly had its challenging moments, but both of you have always looked out for me and "had my back." I am grateful because I know you are there for me always and in every way, and I love you both.

To my beautiful golden boy, Ike (short for *Aikane*, the Hawaiian word for friend). Those who met my amazing dog along the north shore of Kaua`i and those who know me well understand how this sweet animal deeply impacted my life, touched the lives of many others and filled our hearts with joy. He was the true meaning of unconditional love.

Acknowledgments

I would like to recognize and thank the following people for their ongoing support and confidence in me, both personally and professionally. When I had moments of doubt and fear, they reminded me of my brilliance and encouraged me to follow my heart's message.

Thank you to everyone who has helped me along this journey called life . . .

Fran Azouz, Stephanie L.H. Calahan, Cammie Cloman, Joel Comm, Paula D'Andrea, Ava Diamond, Patty Farmer, Andrea Feinberg, Susan Friedmann, Michele Gibson, Tai Goodwin, David Hancock, Peggy Lee Hanson, Lisa Herzlich, Greg Jameson, MJ Jensen, Brian G. Johnson, Nicole Jolie, Amy Kelsall, Arlene Krantz, Deb Krier, Brian Kurtz, Geoff Laughton, Ken McArthur, Terre and Tyler Lantzy, Lianda Ludwig, Kimberly Pitts, Lisa Marie Platske, Laura Rubinstein, the late Eugene Schwartz, Michelle Shaeffer, Patrick Snow, Alice Swanson, Georgina Sweeney, Kathleen Swiderski, Pam Thayer, Tyler Tichelaar, Sindy Wilkinson, and Mark Wood.

Contents

Foreword
by Joel Comm

"You can't make money online," says one person. "It's impossible to do what I love and make a living," says another. A third voice chimes in with, "The economy is too bad for me to start my own business."

What do these three voices all have in common?

They are all wrong . . . horribly wrong.

The problem isn't the people saying these things. It's the mindset that says, "I can't," followed by a list of reasons, more aptly referred to as excuses.

There's no doubt that it takes courage to start your own business.

It takes vision to see how your business can succeed. And it takes someone in tune with the marketing landscape to leverage new media effectively to reach prospects and customers in the hopes of bettering their lives.

That is exactly what Debra Jason has done in her own life. And that's precisely what she is preparing to share with you in this book!

She has demonstrated that it is possible to do what you love, to overcome the obstacles of a sometimes threatening economy and to run a profitable business in the age of social media.

I first met Debra as I was seeking authors for a multi-author book I published in 2013, titled So *What Do You Do? Discovering the Genius Next Door with One Simple Question.* When Debra learned of the project, she communicated her desire to be a part of it. As I got to know her, what I discovered was an incredibly bright, accomplished and passionate woman whose track record speaks for itself!

Her proficiency in copywriting, understanding of social media and heart-driven focus uniquely qualified her to be a part of my project. And now, she has answered the call to pull together her greatest marketing strategies and is delivering them to you in the book you are holding.

The truth is, the time is never better to pursue your dreams than right now!

With the Internet, the barriers of entry for anyone to start a business have never been lower. And with social media, the potential reach for new customers has never been greater.

For those with an entrepreneurial mindset, it's what we call "a perfect storm."

So whether it's overcoming a negative mindset that has some-how kept you stuck in routine for years or decades, or it's getting the direction you need for learning how to market yourself, *Millionaire Marketing on a Shoestring Budget* will answer your questions and get you started on the right foot.

I invite you to jump right in, highlighter in hand (or digital mark-up if you are reading the eBook), and let Debra help put the pieces together for you. I think you'll be inspired as you see the opportunities that lie before you.

And I think Debra would support me in saying this . . . I believe your greatest work lies before you!

Joel Comm
The New York Times Best-Selling Author of *The AdSense Code, Twitter Power 2.0, Click Here to Order, Ka-Ching* and *So What Do You Do?*
www.JoelComm.com

Beating the Odds

"Move out of your comfort zone. You can only grow if you are willing to feel awkward and uncomfortable when you try something new."

— Brian Tracy

Did you know that, according to Small Business Trends, the typical new business started in the United States is no longer in operation five years after being founded?

And, in an article in *Forbes*, according to Bloomberg, 8 out of 10 entrepreneurs who start businesses fail within the first eighteen months. That's right—a whopping 80 percent crash and burn!

It doesn't sound like great odds, but you know what? I believe that if you have a gift you're meant to deliver (and we all do), then you can transform your dream into reality.

This book is your road map to help you achieve that goal—to increase your odds of business success. Use it as your marketing guide, one step at a time. Be creative and do what feels best for you.

If something feels a bit outside your comfort zone, think about it before you decide "I can't do that." Going outside your comfort zone can bring great rewards.

As Neale Donald Walsch says, "Life begins at the end of your comfort zone."

ARE YOU SEEKING GREATER EXPOSURE FOR YOUR BUSINESS?

Do you want to achieve top-of-mind awareness in the marketplace and have a steady stream of loyal, raving fans flocking to you? Are you frustrated because you think you have to spend a lot to get it?

Did you pay a lot of money to design a website, thinking, "If I build it, they will come"? Are you worried because now you're sitting there with no inquiries, no sales?

If you answered, "Yes" to one or all of these questions, I understand your concerns. It can be overwhelming to invest in your business and spend a lot to get yourself up and running, only to scratch your head, wondering, "Why isn't anyone calling me?"

I get it. There's got to be a better way. And the good news is, there is. You can market yourself and your business—in more ways than one—and gain exposure without breaking the bank.

WHY SHOULD YOU LISTEN TO ME?

I started my business from scratch, without a degree in marketing. What I did have was enthusiasm and a desire to succeed. Every suggestion I provide here is one I implemented throughout my years in business. I continue to use these business-building tools on an ongoing basis today.

Since opening my doors, I have delivered hundreds of presentations on the topics of copywriting, marketing and social media marketing; I have written articles for national publications such as *DirectmarketingIQ.com*, *Inside Direct Mail*, *DM News*, *iMarketing News* and *Direct Marketing* magazine; international ones like *Direkt* in Germany; and regional ones like *The Kaua`i Business Report*, *The Denver Business Journal*, *Advertising & Marketing ReView*, *Business Plus* and the *Boulder County Business Report*. And I've been quoted in numerous books on the topics of direct response copywriting and freelancing.

I have taught continuing education classes at the University of Colorado at Boulder and the Professional Development Department at the University of Colorado, and I have been a guest speaker at the undergraduate and graduate level. In addition, I developed the first social media marketing program for the Office of Continuing Education and Training at Kaua`i Community College.

My goal is not only to educate and inspire you, but to *empower* you with the tools you need to communicate your message in a big way. I want you to reach a broader audience, create a flow of happy, raving fans and generate more income, more easily so that you may live the lifestyle you've dreamed about—one that allows you the flexibility, fun and freedom to do what you love with people you love working with.

HOW THE MILLIONAIRE MARKETING PROGRAM CAME ABOUT

Millionaire Marketing on a Shoestring Budget came about shortly after 9-11. Many people were scared and started cutting back on their budgets, and specifically, their marketing budgets.

So in guiding my clients, I compiled a list of affordable ways they could maintain top-of-mind awareness. It's a list of strategies that I implemented during my twenty-five-plus years in business—and I'm still here today, so I am happy to help you discover how to enjoy longevity in your business as well.

As you read the chapters of this book, you will uncover:

- A dozen cost-effective ways to gain exposure for your business—some won't even cost you a dime. That's right; they're FREE!

- The one thing 90 percent of consumers trust more than advertising.

- The best way to market and expose yourself to prospects— without a hard-core sales pitch.

- How to obtain amazing free publicity.

- Seven pointers on how to write a press release that counts.

- One simple step you can take that leads to referrals and new business.

- Six top reasons social media should be in your marketing toolbox.

- How to create allies with colleagues and tap into the power of partnerships.

- One way to find prospects from the comfort of your home— in your PJs or sweats (Hint: It's not social media).

- Eight ideas to charge your batteries and keep your creative juices flowing when you're blogging.

- How to awaken the copywriter within and create headlines that go ka-ching.

- Eight secrets for staying in business happily and successfully for as long as you like.

WHAT ARE YOU WAITING FOR?

I know why you may not have taken action yet. You are busy and scared. You may know some of these strategies, but you lack confidence and are wondering, "Will this work for me?" Perhaps you are a single parent, a work-at-home mom or you're juggling more than one job to make ends meet.

I was once where you are now—feeling overwhelmed, frightened, confused and spinning my wheels. I had a mortgage to pay and no steady salary to support me. I was worried. Now I'm here to help you. I want to relieve you from that anxiety, stress and frustration and motivate you to move forward.

I want to be your marketing muse, mentor and accountability partner. I understand what it is like to get a business off the ground, get the word out to prospects, increase your visibility in the marketplace and keep your customers coming back again and again.

So I have decided to pull back the curtain on my business. I invite you to turn the pages of this book where I reveal how you too can become a seasoned marketing pro running your own business *and* enjoy your life while you are doing it.

After all, the reason you went into business for yourself was to have the freedom-based lifestyle you'd been dreaming about it, isn't it?

ARE YOU READY TO TAKE YOUR BUSINESS TO THE NEXT LEVEL?

This book contains nineteen chapters that deliver creative and cost-effective ideas to inspire you to get your marketing message out there. At the end of each chapter, you'll find an exercise with thought-provoking questions designed to help you start brainstorming and thinking like a seasoned marketer.

I sincerely believe that if I can go from speech pathologist to solopreneur, without a degree in marketing, you too can succeed in pursuing your passion.

As Dale Carnegie suggests in *How to Win Friends and Influence People*, I encourage you to read this book with a highlighter and/or pen in your hand. When you come across a recommendation or a tip that resonates with you, highlight it or make a note in the margin.

"Marking and underscoring a book makes it more interesting and far easier to review rapidly," wrote Carnegie. Then, apply these ideas to your life—personal and professional—at every opportunity.

The highest level of success comes from conviction, commitment and persistence. Are you ready to take your business to the next level? It's time to step outside your comfort zone and succeed in business—in *your* business. Now is the time to let your light shine. Put one foot in front of the other and let's take this journey together and move forward.

Here's to your sweet success,

Debra Jason

Debra Jason

CHAPTER 1

Embracing Change

"If we don't change, we don't grow.
If we don't grow, we aren't really living."

— Gail Sheehy

What does change have to do with marketing? Consider this . . .

If you are in business for yourself and your bank account is not where you want it to be—bills are piling up, the phone isn't ringing and you're worried—then, most likely, you need to change the marketing strategy that you currently have in place.

Or maybe you're trying to build a business in a community where there's no calling for your product or service. You have heard the saying that "Succeeding in business is about location, location, location." At least, that's what it used to be before the Internet.

In today's world, you can live on the island of Kaua`i (like I did), leverage your products and services via the Internet and still be successful. However, at the same time, if you're miserable with where you live, it's not a good fit, you don't like the weather or you haven't found a like-minded community, it may be time for you to move on and that means CHANGE!

I'll admit it; I am not big on making changes in my life. I prefer to keep the status quo rather than shake things up a bit. Perhaps that is why it took me six months to decide to leave Boulder for Kaua`i and then two and a half years for me to reach the decision to return back to Boulder.

HOW DO YOU FEEL ABOUT CHANGE?

I recognize that change is good. While it may take some of us longer to make a change—even if it's painful—it opens the door to new opportunities, new relationships and new adventures.

I've made a few big changes in my life, and I hope by sharing them with you here, you'll realize that even if you are scared, you too can open new doors and move forward.

I am from New York City, the Big Apple—the advertising capital of the country, if not, the world. The funny thing is that, when I graduated college, I went to work at an advertising agency, but I hadn't studied advertising or marketing. I was getting ready to go to graduate school in a different field entirely, but I really liked advertising, so I thought I'd give it a shot. I was not a copywriter then. I was what they called a "floater," doing administrative work in whatever department needed help that day.

In 1976, I decided it was time for graduate school and made a change. I moved to Boulder, Colorado, to get my Master's degree, and I ended up living there after I graduated. I don't have a degree in journalism or English literature. I am a trained and certified speech pathologist with a Master of Arts degree in Communication Disorders.

I worked with children for a few years, and while I loved the kids, I discovered that speech therapy was not my passion.

FINDING YOUR PATH

Have you been in that place? Studied for a degree, worked at a job and realized that the path you were on was not fueling your soul? It took me a while to admit to this. After all, between undergrad and graduate school, I had spent six years studying. When I got physically ill, my body was telling me, "It is time for a change."

Please don't be like me. Don't wait until your body wakes you up with dis-ease.

I found the courage to quit my job without having any idea what I was going to do next. I bought *What Color Is Your Parachute?* and began the exercises outlined in the book. If you've ever read the book, you know it talks about going on information interviews, not job interviews, to research what you might want to do next.

I went from being a speech pathologist to working as a sales representative in the wholesale end of the clothing industry. I love clothes, and purchasing them at below wholesale prices was even a greater benefit, but I was still on a journey.

Fast forward a few years and enter career change number three. Thinking one day it might be cool for me to start my own catalog, I landed a job at a local catalog company. This is where I first started copywriting. I actually worked on the catalog, producing it from start to finish, going to trade shows and looking for products.

After a couple of years in an administrative role, I realized I still was not fueling my passion. I wanted to do something creative. Keep in mind that I had not studied journalism, creative writing or marketing. What I did have, however, was desire. I went to my boss and said, "Let me start writing. If you like the way I write, we'll save money because you won't have to hire a copywriter. And if you don't like the way I write, we'll go back to hiring a copywriter." So bless her heart, she gave me the opportunity to write.

When I was offered a job with a competitor in New York City, since I was born and raised there, I went. New York City is a great place to visit, and having grown up there, I love it. But living back there wasn't the same, and Colorado's blue skies were calling me back.

Because Boulder had been my home for many years, you may be thinking, "Returning there was not a change, Debra," but believe me, making the decision to move was not an easy one. It was scary because I had no job to return to in Boulder.

Hence, career change number four: I returned to Boulder in 1988, when times were tough—really tough. I went out looking for a job because I still didn't know at that time that I was going to start my own business.

The reason I went out on my own was because people were getting laid off at all the agencies I approached. I was caught in the Colorado recession and repeatedly heard, "Sorry; we're not hiring. We're laying people off right now, Debra."

BELIEVE IN YOURSELF

If you've been looking—or were looking—for a J-O-B, this scenario may sound all too familiar. It is a tough place to be.

I was petrified back then. How was I going to pay my bills, not to mention my mortgage? Here I was back in a place I loved, with friends I loved, but no job in place. Talk about scary. I think there are people out there reading this book who know just what I am talking about. Maybe you're one of them.

But then, it struck me like a lightning bolt.

Because, in addition to "We're laying people off right now," many of the people who interviewed me also said, "Debra, we can't hire you as an employee, but if you were to freelance, we could use your services."

I took this as a sign from above—it was my opportunity to grab the bull by the horns and start my own business. I had always said that I wanted my own business, but I never knew what that business was going to be. So I made a decision and opened my own copywriting business. On January 1st, 1989, The Write Direction was born.

Now, what I'd like you to keep in mind is that I—perhaps like you—had no clients. Many freelance copywriters start their businesses after working at an agency, and they have clients who follow along with them.

In a blog post, a fellow copywriter wrote that he worked at an agency and when it went belly up, he went on his own and found himself with a boatload of new clients who went with him from the agency.

But that wasn't me. I had to start from scratch—no clients and a very limited portfolio. Sound risky? It absolutely was!

However, despite the Colorado recession, I was able to break ground, make an impact, find clients and establish a successful business.

I am telling you these details because all of it happened as a result of a concerted effort to market myself and keep marketing. I stress this because many people have been working really hard for a long time and now they're feeling deflated and aren't sure where to turn to next. Maybe that's the reason why you picked up this book!

I know how it feels—believe me. When I started my business, I sent out direct mail letters, networked like crazy and followed up with phone calls. I'd take it personally when people said, "No thanks, Debra."

It can be hard not to take it personally. I don't know about you, but I take many things personally that I shouldn't. But you know, there I was banging on doors and people were saying, "No," and I was thinking, "I must be crazy. I must be crazy to do this."

What I will tell you is that I was consistent and very persistent. I believed in myself and did not give up—and here it is twenty-five-plus years later. It's not like I didn't have those days when I was in tears, where I thought, "What am I doing?" I certainly did, but I kept going. And, gratefully, I had the help and support of dear friends, family members and colleagues who saw me through many up and down times.

Here's one of my favorite quotes about being persistent. It is from Calvin Coolidge. He said:

"Nothing in the world can take the place of persistence. Talent will not; nothing is more common than unsuccessful men with talent. Genius will not; unrewarded genius is almost a proverb. Education will not; the world is full of educated derelicts. Persistence and determination alone are omnipotent."

I wrote this book because I wanted to take my two-plus decades of experiences and share them with you to let you know that *you* too can do it.

There is a reason I was able to go back and forth from Colorado to New York and then Colorado to Kaua`i. (I lived on the island of Kaua`i for ten years.) I'm living a different lifestyle than I *ever* had when I worked for an employer.

I advise you to do the same. If you are changing direction in your life—on a new path—hold on, keep up the good work and you *will* achieve your goals. I'm not saying it's easy, but it can be very rewarding. Now is the time to let your light shine and live your dream.

DON'T BE AFRAID OF CHANGE—IT'S NEVER TOO LATE

Have you ever watched *The X Factor*? In one episode, country singer Tate Stevens was a contestant. He had always wanted to sing, but he had put his dreams aside to raise a family. When he was age thirty-seven, his family encouraged him to pursue his singing career and audition for *The X Factor*. He thought he was too old to pursue his dream, but he decided to go for it anyway. And guess what? *He won a $5 million recording contract!*

You see, it is never too late to go for it and pursue your dreams. Reading this book is a step in that direction—in the right direction.

I changed my career several times and you can too. You can do whatever you want to do. Just because you don't have a college degree in a certain field doesn't mean you can't change your career.

If a speech pathologist can succeed in marketing, I don't care what career you're in now, you too can succeed in marketing—as long as you have the desire and are willing to learn.

"The only way to make sense out of change is to plunge into it, move with it, and join the dance."

— Alan Watts

EXERCISE:

Take some quiet time for yourself. Think about where you are now. Answer these questions below.

Are you happy or are you considering a change?

_____

Have you made any big changes in your life recently? What are they?

_____

_____

_____

_____

_____

What happened when you made the change?

_____

_____

_____

_____

If money were not an issue and you could do whatever you wanted, what would you choose?

_____

_____

_____

_____

Other than money, is there anything else stopping you?

_____

_____

_____

_____

CHAPTER 2

Gaining Exposure for Your Business—You Can Do It Cost-Effectively

"One of the most common false economies (i.e., saving money in the wrong way) is cutting back on marketing itself . . . which means a probable loss of the investment in awareness that you've already made . . . . To terminate your marketing investment to save money is like stopping your wristwatch to save time."

— Jay Conrad Levinson

Are you getting the lion's share of business?

In the first chapter, we talked about change. Well, in 2001, the country was faced with a big change—the after effects of September 11th. Even before the tragic events of 9-11 rolled around, the economy was heading in a downward spiral. Then again, in 2008, the country found itself dealing with a weakened economy, daily gloom and doom news headlines and, hence, more turbulent times.

MARKETING IN TURBULENT TIMES

When times get tough, many companies make a change in the form of cutbacks. Sometimes, they let employees go; other times, they eliminate their marketing. "A bad move," said Colorado communications pro Stacy Cornay. "The public has to be reminded about who you are and what you're selling . . . . Instead of cutting back on marketing, be more aggressive."

Public relations pro John Shors wrote, "When companies cease touting themselves via the media, opportunities are created for their competitors to step into the spotlight . . . ."

A year after September 11th, professionals like B2B telemarketing consultant Michael Brown said, "It's not quite 'full steam ahead,' but notwithstanding the turbulent economy, people feel that they can't not market."

When hit with hard times, it can take time for people to bounce back. But there are also those people who continue to thrive despite the bad news. They stay focused and plunge forward with top-of-mind marketing so that they maintain a presence and are not easily forgotten.

Fast forward to 2008 when Michael Beck of ClientMonkey.com explained, "It might even be tempting to 'ride it out' . . . to do nothing until things turn around. This passive approach yields passive results. Nothing will happen while you're waiting and when things do turn around, the business will go to the people who've been doing something all along. The people who will get the lion's share of the business—both now and in the future—are the ones who work to build relationship."

EVEN WHEN TIMES ARE TOUGH, YOU CAN GET THE LION'S SHARE OF BUSINESS

As I mentioned, I started my business in 1989, when times were tough in Colorado. The reason I went out on my own was because people were getting laid off at all the agencies I approached. I was caught in the Colorado recession and repeatedly heard, "Sorry; we're not hiring. We're laying people off right now."

I could have seen this as defeat. Instead, I took this as a "sign from above." A lightbulb went off—it was my opportunity to grab the bull by the horns and go out on my own.

Despite a recession, I was able to break ground . . . make an impact . . . find clients . . . establish a successful business. As stated earlier, it happened because of a concerted effort to market myself and keep marketing. I encourage you to do the same.

You may need to re-evaluate what you have been doing to get your name out there. You may need to shift your focus and change your plan of action. But remember, as we discussed in Chapter 1, embracing change can be a good thing. If you have a dream you want realized, instead of pulling back in fear, plow forward with focus.

"In these cash-tight times, marketing budgets and brand-building activities are often the first cost centers to get the axe. But rather than slashing the budget and crossing your fingers, refocusing your marketing and brand-building initiatives can help you stay top-of-mind with customers," said Anthony Pappas, CEO of the Pappas Group.

ARE YOU STAYING A STEP AHEAD OF YOUR COMPETITION?

Whether the economy is slow or you're just getting started in your business, it can be frightening to dip into your budget. But to stay ahead of your competition, marketing should be an ongoing priority for your company.

Janet Attard, founder of the *Business Know How* website, suggests that you "Understand the importance of marketing and learn how to do it effectively. The world won't beat a path to your door just because you build a better mousetrap or write a great ebook about how to grow tomatoes or teach a child to read. To get customers you will have to market your products or services effectively and continually."

She goes on to say, "Don't expect miracles. Yes, people do make money in their sleep or while they're away on vacation—the Internet makes that possible. But only after they've invested a lot of time, effort, and money in building the business and building the team that keeps it going and growing."

Good advice, but do not be scared. You can market yourself without spending three million dollars for a thirty-second Super Bowl commercial. How?

Keep reading. This book guides you through more than a dozen cost-effective marketing tools you can add to your marketing toolbox so that you:

1. Don't let people forget who you are . . . where you are . . . how you can be reached.
2. Do what you can to maintain a presence.

3. Stay in touch with your customers, be it via phone, "snail" mail or email and ask them what they want and need.

If you are visible, when your competition is not, your marketing efforts will invite potential customers to call *you!*

EXERCISE:

What steps are you currently taking to market yourself?

_____

_____

_____

What makes you different from your competition?
How do you stand out?

_____

_____

_____

Do you have a marketing budget?
If so, where are you putting those dollars?

_____

_____

_____

CHAPTER 3

Understanding Two Vital Keys to Successful Marketing

"Our job is to connect to people, to interact with them in a way that leaves them better than we found them, more able to get where they'd like to go."

— Seth Godin

In the last chapter, we discussed that you don't need to have a Super Bowl budget to gain exposure for your business. While you do not need to spend a fortune, you do need to spend time preparing. There are two key elements you must have a solid grasp on *before* planning your marketing campaign or writing any content:

1. Your Product
2. Your Market

DO YOU KNOW THE ANSWERS TO THESE QUESTIONS?

Believe it or not, I have found that one mistake people often make is not knowing—*really* knowing—their program/product/service or their target market. (NOTE: Throughout the book when I mention "product," I'm referring to a product, service, or program you may be promoting.)

When I started my business more than twenty-five years ago, I had a client who, when I started asking him questions about his business, said, "If I could answer that, I wouldn't need you to write this for me!"

While it might be fun to read people's minds, sorry folks, copywriters and consultants are not mind readers. You are working as a team, so it is important to collaborate.

To gain a thorough understanding of what your product is, ask yourself these questions *before* you ever start marketing.

1. What is the physical product? You may say, "I don't have a physical product; I'm teaching a program online." Well, that program may include an hour webinar, five modules, CDs, white papers, recordings of live sessions. Get the picture?

2. What is the functional product? What does the product do? What problem does it solve for your clients? What are the benefits that your product performs? Keep in mind that features are different than benefits (see question number five).

3. What is your goal?

- To sell more product? If so, how much?
- To gain name recognition?
- To build your brand—create an image?
- To generate leads?

- To introduce a new product or an improvement of an old one?

4. What is the single strongest benefit that harnesses the greatest sales power at a particular point in time? This is what is known as the USP (unique selling proposition). In other words, how will you touch people's emotions and "knock their socks off"?

Some marketers tell you to "tap into your prospects' pain." I call it "pushing your prospects' buttons." While they're reading your content, your prospects should find themselves saying, "Yeah! That's me. Yes, this person understands the challenges I face. I need this program now!"

5. What will your product do for "me"? "Me" refers to your prospect or customer. List the benefits of your product versus its features. For example, a feature = six 1-hour modules. The benefit = "This program generates ten new leads for you each week."

6. Why should I buy your product over someone else's? What will buyers of your product expect or perceive they are getting? Is it worth it? What makes you different?

7. What objections might there be to your product (i.e., cost, time)? You may have noticed that many training programs online offer payment plans to overcome the cost objection. Others offer recordings to overcome time objections (i.e., listen at your own pace and convenience). If there is a possible objection or barrier to your product, you may want to address it in your marketing content.

IT'S TIME FOR A TEST

Relax, you won't be judged or graded on this. I think you'll pass with flying colors. It's called The Pencil Test. If you have a pencil nearby, grab it. If not, just use your imagination. Pretend you're holding a pencil.

Now, what I'd like you to do is:

a. Write down the features of the pencil. For example, it has an eraser.

b. Convert those features into benefits. The feature is it has an eraser, but the benefit is that you can write stress-free, without worrying about making mistakes because you can always erase them and start over again.

c. After you have written down the obvious benefits, stretch your imagination and see what else you can come up with that's a "not-so-obvious" benefit. When I give this exercise during a live presentation, we do it in groups and attendees really have fun with this one.

For instance, when they think "outside the box," one benefit groups have come up with for an eraser is that—for those who wear earrings—when you lose the back of one, you can use the eraser as a temporary replacement for that earring back.

Go beyond the obvious. The reason I ask you to do this exercise is to get your creative juices flowing. When you think "I can't think of more benefits of my business/service, I just keep coming up with features,"—give yourself some time and just brainstorm.

Don't censor what comes up. Let it flow and put whatever you think of first down on paper. Start with features, convert them into benefits and then go beyond the obvious. I know it sounds cliché, but think outside the box.

If you are in a Mastermind group, ask your colleagues to brainstorm with you. Or gather a group of trusted friends together and have fun with it. You may be pleasantly surprised by all the great ideas you generate together—more than if you did this exercise by yourself.

DO YOU KNOW YOUR IDEAL CLIENT?

In addition to knowing your product, it is vital that you understand who makes up your target audience before you begin marketing. What keeps these people awake at night and how can you help them?

Speaking to everyone is like speaking to no one. Be sure you know who it is you want to speak to. For instance, many weight-loss and/or fitness coaches will say, "My ideal clients are women." However, it is important to drill down even deeper. Are they women who:

- Are obese and want to lose more than thirty pounds?
- Just had a baby and are struggling to lose those last five pounds?
- Are getting ready for their wedding days and want to lose weight so they'll look fabulous in their wedding gowns?

Do you see how you would approach each of these female audiences differently when writing your copy?

Here are some questions you might ask yourself to gain clarity about your target audience:

1. What is the market's mass desire (the public spread of a private want)?

Examples:

- The desire of men to be virile and strong.
- The desire of women to be attractive and slim.
- The desire of both men and women to keep their health.

When you're addressing your ideal client (be it in a brochure, direct mail piece or website), your job is to take this mass desire and direct it, channel it and focus it onto your product or service.

2. What are the market demographics? Age, sex, education, income, career, marital status. However, keep in mind that career may not be as important as the qualities or values you seek in your ideal client.

In his book *Content Warfare*, Ryan Hanley shared that according to a 2013 Brand Engagement Survey done by Gensler, 87 percent of consumers choose brands that match their values. And 71 percent of consumers will not buy from brands whose values go against their own. Values fall under psychographics, which leads us to question number three.

3. What are the psychographics? What are the lifestyles of your ideal clients like? Is family important to them? Are they cramped for time? What do they like to do in their free time? Do they use credit cards often? Do they dine out or like to stay at home and eat in? Do they have a history of investing to get help for their problem(s)?

4. What motivates your audience? Can you describe the problems/needs/issues/challenges they are facing on a daily basis? What has them tossing and turning when they get in bed at night? Are they motivated to solve their problems?

5. Are they findable? Do you know where they like to congregate or hang out? Can they be reached easily?

VISUALIZING YOUR IDEAL CLIENT

I'd like you to play along with me here and do a creative visualization. You might want to take a moment to record the instructions below so you can play it back later without having to refer to the book.

First, sit in a comfortable position. Then, close your eyes. Now take a deep breath, hold it for a moment and exhale. Do this two more times. Settle in and relax.

Next, I'd like you to imagine you are at your local coffee shop or teahouse, and while you're waiting in line to place your order, you overhear the customer in front of you. She is talking to the barista about her day. It's been troublesome, and as you listen, you hear her describing exactly the problem or need your product fulfills.

Listen to her carefully. As you do, she talks about all the issues that your product can solve! Imagine what you think your perfect prospect would say in this situation and how you might respond.

Give yourself some time to imagine the details of this situation. How does the conversation play out in your mind?

When the conversation is over, it's time to end the visualization. Before opening your eyes, take a deep breath, hold it, and exhale. Do that two more times.

Then, when you are ready, open your eyes. Before you do anything else, pick up a pen and write down what happened in your visualization.

Do it now, while it's fresh in your mind.

_____

_____

_____

_____

That customer you visualized had a problem he/she couldn't handle. You have the solution. As you visualized that conversation in your mind, you probably got several ideas on how to approach your marketing in the future. And the reward? You now have some excellent copy points to use in your marketing materials.

WHAT IS YOUR MARKET'S STATE OF AWARENESS?

The next component to keep in mind, with regard to knowing your audience, is to understand their state of awareness—the awareness that they have a problem and that you have a great way to solve it for them.

My mentor, the late Eugene Schwartz, talks about four different levels of awareness in his book _Breakthrough Advertising_. If you can get your hands on a copy, you should; it's one of the "bibles" in the direct marketing world. You might find it on Amazon. If not, contact the original publisher, Boardroom Books; they reprint it on occasion.

State of Awareness means: What is the market's present state of knowledge about your product and the satisfaction that your product performs?

1. Fully Aware - They know about your product—what it does—and know that they want it. This is the easiest market to talk to.

2. Not Completely Aware - They know about your product but aren't completely aware of everything it does, or are not convinced of how well it does it, or haven't yet been told how much better it does it now.

3. Less aware - They either know or recognize immediately that they want what the product does, but they don't yet know that there is a product—your product—that will do it for them.

4. Completely unaware (as you might guess, this is the most difficult market to address) - they are either not aware of their desire or need—or they won't honestly admit it to themselves without being led into it by your sales page—or the need is their own secret that just can't be verbalized yet.

This is where one headline to one state of awareness might work to convert one prospect, but not another prospect who is at a different level of awareness.

For instance, someone like Tony Robbins has built a loyal following. Therefore, many people he promotes to are aware of his programs and services. They recognize that he delivers solutions—so they're easier to market to because of their familiarity with him.

Your business may be new to the market and require more relationship building with your prospects. Now, it's your job to help them become aware that you have a solution to their problem.

"No marketing succeeds if it can't find an audience that already wants to believe the story being told."

— Seth Godin

EXERCISE:

Before you begin marketing or writing any of your marketing materials, it is important that you have a thorough understanding of two key elements: your product and your market.

What is your product/program/service?

_____

_____

_____

What is the single strongest benefit of your product (the benefit that harnesses the strongest selling power)?

_____

_____

Who is your ideal client? Do you love working with him/her?

_____

_____

_____

_____

_____

_____

_____

What objection/barrier might he/she have to your product, if any?

_____

_____

_____

_____

_____

_____

Fill in the blanks of this formula and you'll have a thirty-second *spiel* that helps you clarify and communicate who it is you help and how you help them with your product:

I help (insert target audience) _____

Do, get or gain (insert benefit) _____

Even if (insert an objection/barrier) _____

So that (insert a result/benefit) _____

CHAPTER 4

Taking a Leadership Role in Your Life

"Nothing will work unless you do."

— Maya Angelou

O n the previous pages, we explored the importance of understanding your product and your target market. Once you have a clear picture of whom you serve and how you can help them, it is time to get your message out there and gain exposure for your business.

Do you know the one simple step you can take that leads to referrals and new business?

In their book *Marketing Your Service Business*, authors Jean Withers and Carol Vipperman wrote: "Joining just two organizations of people who might be prospective clients can provide referrals and new business . . . . Ask associates which organizations might be most suitable for you. Visit the organizations before you decide to join."

Joining professional organizations—making connections face-to-face—is a great way to start marketing yourself and your business. However, don't just pay your membership dues and walk away.

DON'T JUST JOIN—GET INVOLVED!

There are so many people in business who want get-rich-quick marketing strategies. They hope they can wave a magic wand and make a million dollars by the afternoon.

While that sounds great, the first thing you have to realize is that you must take a leadership role in your business and execute. You must take action. If you don't do it, nobody else is going to do it for you. One of my eight secrets for success (see Chapter 19) is taking responsibility for yourself.

One way to do that is to get involved in professional organizations. The reason why you want to get involved is to network. And the reason you want to network is because your net worth is determined by the size of your network.

"All the answers that you seek can be found in the people whom you know or whom you are willing to meet," says small business coach Patrick Snow.

YOUR NET WORTH IS DETERMINED BY YOUR NETWORK

Many people join organizations, sit back and wait for business to come their way. I can't tell you how many times I've heard something like this, "Well, I joined the Chamber, but it hasn't done anything for me." Clients don't automatically knock on your door just because you have become a member of your Chamber of Commerce or the local chapter of the ABC Association.

When I started my business, I made the decision to join two professional organizations. I chose one that was in my local community

(Chamber of Commerce) and one that was within my industry (Rocky Mountain Direct Marketing Association).

Taking a leadership role in my life, I did not sit back. I joined and quickly got involved in each community. Among other things, I served as the committee chair for the Small Business Support Council and Business Women's Leadership Group as well as served on the Board of Directors at the Boulder Chamber of Commerce. When I moved to Kaua`i, after I had been involved in a variety of organizations, I was invited to Chair the Women in Business Roundtable and served as President of the Kaua`i North Shore Business Council.

As a result of this involvement, I met amazing people. And over time, many of these people helped me out, referred me to colleagues, asked me to speak at events and more.

For example, my involvement in the Rocky Mountain Direct Marketing Association (RMDMA) led me to become its newsletter editor, board member and eventually, President of the Board. During one of our annual events, I became friends and colleagues with the keynote speaker, and today, we are doing business together.

I arranged for him to speak to two different organizations when I lived on Kaua`i. Several years later, when we re-connected in Colorado, he encouraged and helped me get this book out of my head and onto paper.

If I hadn't attended that meeting back in 2009, where he and I met, then there's a chance that this book may have never been published. Just by taking a leadership role in my life, joining the RMDMA, networking, eventually becoming a President of the organization, and meeting a lot of people, I am now a published author.

ARE YOU TAKING A LEADERSHIP ROLE IN YOUR LIFE?

Once you've joined an organization, why not volunteer to serve on a committee (i.e., public relations, entertainment, programming, event planning, etc.) or sit on the Board of Directors?

I strongly believe that this is where you begin to make more valuable connections and expand your community. By doing so, fellow colleagues find out who you are on a more personal level, learn more about your business and discover your capabilities.

You increase your network of contacts and are given the chance to share your expertise. Before you know it, you may find an email in your inbox or your phone rings and the person contacting you is someone you never met. However, that person is connected to someone you know, and that person referred you because he or she enjoyed working on a committee or Board with you.

WHICH GROUPS TO JOIN?

In *Marketing Your Consulting and Professional Services*, Dick Connor and Jeffrey Davidson maintain that "Visit any metro area and attend a local meeting of the Red Cross, International Rotary . . . or other civic, professional, or charitable groups and undoubtedly, you will meet many of the area's most successful professionals. Successful professionals know that giving of their time freely is an excellent way to be of service to the community and to help build the firm."

Consider these opportunities:

- Business Networking International (BNI)

- Business and Professional Women (BPW)

- Chamber of Commerce

- Rotary International Club

- Zonta International (organization for professional women)

- Your local business associations (When I lived on Kaua`i, there was the Kaua`i North Shore Business Council, Kapaa Business Association, Women in Business Roundtable.)

- Fundraising or non-profit organizations

- National Association of Women Business Owners (NAWBO)

- Local advertising or direct marketing clubs

- Local marketing or public relations associations

- Local Meetup groups (meetup.com)

- Toastmasters International®

NETWORKING—IT'S NOT ABOUT COLLECTING BUSINESS CARDS

Please keep in mind that when you attend these meetings, networking is not all about collecting business cards. It's about beginning to build relationships!

My colleague and business growth strategist Patty Farmer said she lives by this quote, "Strive to be a people connector, not a business card collector." It's definitely advice worth living by.

Your first question shouldn't be, "May I have your card?" Ask thought-provoking questions and be a good listener. Keep in mind that when you show a genuine interest in others, they'll find you interesting.

As a young salesman, Harvey Mackay, author of *Swim with the Sharks without Being Eaten Alive*, developed the Mackay 66™—a sixty-six-question customer profile that focuses on what makes people tick. For instance, what are they proud of accomplishing? What's their life like outside the office? How do they want to be seen by others? If you want to see the exact sixty-six questions, simply search "Mackay 66" online.

Here are four characteristics of successful networkers from Jeffrey Gitomer. He said you need:

- A heartfelt introduction (what I call the "thirty-second *spiel*"—see the exercise in Chapter 3) that engages and encourages listeners to ask more.
- A willingness to dedicate the time it takes to network and be good at it.
- A plan of where and when to network.
- To know which events to attend where your customers and prospects are likely to go.

When you are at a networking event and take time to get to know someone, the moment may naturally come when you do exchange business cards. When it does, be sure to follow up. After all, how will you develop a relationship if you just tuck that card in a drawer?

On the back of the business card, write down one or two points from your conversation and, after the event, do one (or more) of the following:

1. Send a handwritten note. People will appreciate the time you took to sit down and write. Perhaps they spoke with you about their child's soccer game or a vacation that is approaching. Mention it again in your note.

It's rare for most of us to receive personal "snail" mail these days, so it is quickly noticed in one's mailbox. You can send an email, but I find the handwritten note makes a lasting impression. And, with so few people doing this, you will stand out from the crowd.

2. Connect with that person on LinkedIn. However, please don't send him or her one of LinkedIn's generic invitations. Take the time to personalize the invite and reiterate a point you discussed when you met. It's a great way to continue your conversation and start building relationships. Read more about LinkedIn in Chapter 11.

3. Check out the person's website, read her blog and see whether she's on other social networks (i.e., Facebook, Twitter, Google Plus, etc.). If so, connect with the person there as well. Or better yet, do what Networking CEO Patty Farmer does. When meeting someone for the first time and obtaining her business card, she asks that person how she would like to connect. Patty then folds a corner of her business card to represent her preferred social network. If she says Google Plus, Patty folds the upper right corner, Facebook is the lower right corner, Twitter the lower left and LinkedIn the upper left. Later on, she'll take out the business card and connect with that person according to her preference. A great idea you can implement right away.

START YOUR OWN NETWORKING GROUP

When marketing and branding strategist Kimberly Pitts started feeling like networking was a waste of time, she made a decision to start her own Meetup groups. She was assertive—she did not wait for her ideal clients to find her. She focused on connecting and getting to know them, building the KLT Factor (i.e., know, like and trust) along the way.

"I held fun events in creative locations and taught marketing principles at each meeting," explained Kimberly. "I structured each event to be more than just meeting up and socializing. I infused learning into each one—presenting ideas about marketing and branding in each meeting. These events were very crucial in developing my business, because I helped others see that marketing your business is fun, creative and it should be designed around who you are."

In addition, when she started her business U Impact, LLC, Kimberly hosted launch events at local restaurants where there was no cost to use their meeting rooms. "I'd ask five to seven people I knew well to support me in getting the word out," she explained. Committed to helping her, they spread the word to others who fit her ideal client profile.

Then, when people attended, she made sure it was very interactive—no heavy selling whatsoever. And she made a point to get to know those in attendance. She shared what her business was with them, and she learned what they were striving to do. This helped them get to know her and vice versa. As a result, they would then refer their friends to the next gathering she held.

To date, Kimberly still hosts these networking get-togethers because they continue to be an effective tool for her business. "My biggest cost was just time, but it was well worth it."

Patty Farmer started a Facebook networking group targeted specifically toward global speakers, radio show hosts, authors, publishers and media experts. She set very clear parameters on how members should interact within the group (i.e., no sales pitches). She made it clear that the group was about serving one another, keeping it high value, high integrity and a place for discussion on strategies, opportunities and the celebrations of each members' success.

"I monitor the group closely so it stays focused on serving each other and keeping the posts targeted to authors and speakers," explained Patty. Since starting the group, Patty has been booked for more than sixty speaking engagements. And I have spoken on numerous Blog Talk Radio shows, podcasts and webinars as the result of my participation in the group as well.

I hope you're inspired by this chapter and your "wheels are turning" thinking about where you can step up, reach out and get involved. When you do, I am optimistic that you will discover the benefits of taking a leadership role in your life and view networking on a whole new level.

> *"I've learned that people will forget what you said,*
> *people will forget what you did,*
> *but people will never forget how you made them feel."*
>
> —Maya Angelou

EXERCISE:

What are your areas of interest/expertise?

_____

_____

_____

_____

_____

_____

_____

_____

Write down two questions you might ask someone the first time you meet at a networking event.

1. _____

2. _____

Research groups/organizations in your area and write down 2-3 you want to investigate further.

1. _____

2. _____

3. _____

Search LinkedIn and Facebook for groups that are beneficial for you. Write them down here:

_____

_____

_____

_____

_____

_____

_____

CHAPTER 5

Standing in the Spotlight—the Most Fun Way to Market Yourself

"When I speak, business happens."

— Bob Moawad

A popular question many of us heard throughout our childhoods was, "What do you want to be when you grow up?" Remember when you finally realized the answer to this question? How excited you were and how you wished that someone would give you your big break?

Perhaps you wanted to be a movie star or a rock 'n roll musician.

For me, it was an actress. As early as elementary school, I wanted to (and did) act. I played Amaryllis in *The Music Man*, one of the Von Trapp kids in *The Sound of Music*, and sang and danced in *Brigadoon*.

I loved the spotlight . . . the attention . . . the music and dancing.

Then, I wanted to be a model—another career that would put me in the spotlight. Think I liked the idea of being the center of attention?

Guess so.

However, things didn't go as I had hoped. After the High School of Performing Arts turned me down and New York modeling agencies said I was too short, I gave up on those childhood dreams.

Today, although you won't see me at the Academy Awards accepting an Oscar or on the cover of a fashion magazine, as a speaker and author, I get to live out the childhood dream of standing in the spotlight.

The tip I deliver in this chapter is one of my favorites. In my opinion, it is the best and most fun way to market yourself and get exposure among your prospects without a hard sale approach. Just be yourself.

SPEAKING IN PUBLIC

"The best way to market yourself is to give yourself to the market. Expose yourself to your prospects," wrote Jeffrey Gitomer. And I add that public speaking is an engaging, interactive way to market yourself. You're out there, among people, connecting eye-to-eye and face-to-face.

It means a lot to me, when I am speaking, to see people's faces, watch their reactions and have them participate in exercises as well as asking questions. There's energy in the room that fuels them and me.

The benefits of giving public speeches (speeches, not sales pitches) are you:

- Get to give a live sales presentation to sell yourself, not your product or service. Just yourself.
- Get to do an audition right in front of decision makers.
- Build and strengthen your network.

- Establish your presence.
- Help the community. That's a great thing.
- Develop your speaking skills.
- Get to try out new material.
- Attract new customers.
- Have a meaningful impact on someone through your words.

Keynote speaker and founder of Big Impact Speaking, Ava Diamond, said, "I think speaking is the fastest way for entrepreneurs to get clients and cash into their business. It's really critical that they get out and speak."

My mission has been to educate, inspire and empower solo- and entrepreneurs as well as small business professionals. Therefore, I know I'm having a positive effect on them when I receive comments like these from attendees:

"I loved your session today! You are so comfortable being exactly who you are and sharing yourself with everyone in the room. Thank you. I appreciate that you emphasized . . . it's all about relationships . . . and there is no greater marketing plan than "who we are" . . . . You are such an inspiration." — T. Asanti, Heritage Title Co., Eagle, CO

"Thank you so much. I was so inspired and energized . . . . You know it's a great program when you leave feeling so good. I really enjoyed it. You are very good at what you do." — I. Peplinski, RE/MAX Vail Valley, Edwards, CO

"Thank you for a well-done presentation and for being so enthusiastic; it was inspiring." — C. Canale, Village Makeover, Boulder, CO

Feedback like this warms my heart and inspires me to keep on doing what I do. You too can have the same effect on people when you get out and speak!

BUILDING YOUR AUTHORITY

Sharing what you know increases your credibility regarding your area of expertise. And speaking at meetings puts you among a circle of business people who may need your services—if not right away, perhaps at a later date.

When I spoke on a Chamber of Commerce panel about direct mail, I ended up with a new client and several prospects. After speaking to members of the Greater Denver Postal Customer Council about integrating direct mail and social media, I ended up with two new clients.

Andrea Feinberg, President of Coaching Insight, agrees that public speaking is a marketing tool that validates her audience's impression of her. "I'm in a business that provides tangible results through service delivery. Part of that service implies having a relationship with me; whether someone works with me as their executive coach, they buy my book or an e-program, it's all delivered through my point of view and expertise.

"So, using marketing tools that reveal what it might be like is important. The more I can do that through live or recorded presentations, the more someone is likely to want to know more (and then opt in for a free offer) or it will validate their impression of me and they'll make a purchase."

In offering five reasons why entrepreneurs should consider public speaking as a marketing tool, Ava Diamond's number one reason is about building authority as well.

She said, "When you're in front of the room, in the minds of the people in that audience, you're the undisputed authority on your topic. Because not only do you bring whatever credibility you have to the table, but you also have the credibility of whatever organization has invited you there to speak. While there may only be 100 people in that room, the organization may have a mailing list of a thousand or multiple thousands of people who now see your name as the undisputed authority on your topic. I think that is a really cool thing."

THE "BOMB" FOR BRINGING IN CLIENTS AND CASH FAST

Here are four additional reasons Ms. Diamond believes entrepreneurs should consider public speaking as a marketing tool for their businesses:

1. You are in front of an audience comprised of your perfect target clients. Normally, in the course of a day those people have a zillion things competing for their attention. They are texting, emailing and doing whatever they're doing so they are multi-focused," explained Ava.

"When you're in front of the room, they're sitting there watching YOU. If you are any good, their only focus is going to be on you. You have 20, 50 or 100 people of your ideal clients with all of their attention focused on you. That's a bonanza in my opinion," Ava continued.

2. Speaking is the fastest way to build know, like and trust. And Ava loves what Internet Pioneer Joel Comm added to this. He said it's not just know, like and trust. It's know me, like me, trust me, pay me. "I love that addition (pay me) and it's true. If you're making an offer, they may not take you up on your offer that day, but you can

get them on your list and build a relationship with them. Your goal is that the 'pay me' will come at some point or another because you built the know, like and trust factor first. The 'pay' follows that with time," Ava stressed.

"And, with in-person speaking, there's just not any better way to build that know, like, and trust because people experience you face-to-face. Now, some are going to love you and some are going to hate you, if you're provocative at all (which you want to be). You want to have a point of view, so everybody's not going to love you, but the people who resonate with your message are going to be raving fans if you're any good."

3. Speaking really lets you sell without selling. If you're in the spirit of service, it lets you make an offer to your ideal clients that will fix a problem in their life so you can sell without being pushy. *Yes, you can sell without being pushy.* You can, if you construct your speech well, just lead people to a solution to their problem—a problem that you have identified and they have related to in the course of listening to you speak.

4. The "bomb" for bringing clients and cash in fast, is that if you were to talk to let's say fifty prospects individually, even if you only talked to each one for a half hour, that would take you twenty-five hours. As a speaker, you can talk to all those fifty people in one hour. It is time effective.

Then, if you are going to have one-on-one follow up calls with people, you're only following up with people who raised their hands and said, "Yes, I want to speak with you about working with you." It's a lot more productive to talk to those ten than to talk to all fifty people, forty of whom might not be interested at all.

So that's it in a nutshell—why Ava thinks, "Any entrepreneur who is not getting out and speaking is nuts because there are at least four darn good reasons to get out there."

GATHERING ENDORSEMENTS AND REFERRALS

Ava says, "One of the key things you want to do when you speak is to get leads, referrals and testimonials from your audience. You've given them great value and now they have an opportunity to give back to you." But how do you get all three?

When you're not being paid to speak, Ava suggests that you use an evaluation form and include these three sections in it:

Section 1 – Collecting testimonials

a) What would you tell other people about this program you attended today?

b) What would you say about (insert your name) as a speaker? May I quote you? If so, please provide your name and organization. (NOTE: I often let people know that if they prefer, I'll use their first initial and last name or just their initials along with their city and state.)

Section 2 – Collecting leads and referrals

Ava says that, on her form, she has a big headline there that reads "I'd like to stay connected with Ava!" Under that, there are spaces for the attendees to insert his or her name, email and phone number along with four choices as follows:

1. Please subscribe me to your newsletter.

2. Please contact me regarding scheduling a possible presentation,

workshop or training.

3. I have a referral and/or business opportunity for (insert your name) and would like to be contacted to discuss this further.

4. Comments.

Section 3 – Offering a complimentary session

Offer attendees the opportunity to schedule a complimentary coaching/consulting call with you. This is a good way to pursue a conversation and see whether the potential exists for you to work together on a deeper level.

If you're being paid to speak, you only need sections one and two on your form.

In order to ensure a higher rate of return of people turning in the evaluation form, consider offering the audience members a bonus handout related to the topic you spoke about. When they leave the room, they can hand in their forms and, as a "thank you," you give them your information-packed bonus report, tip sheet, or handout on their way out.

I've acquired testimonials, leads and referrals two ways:

1. An evaluation form at the end of a presentation as Ava suggested.

2. A follow-up email that I send attendees after the presentation, along with a bonus, and I ask them for their feedback at that time.

I have a simple template I use when I make these requests. Visit my website at: www.writedirection.com/testimonial-approach and request a copy. I'll be happy to send it your way.

DON'T WAIT TO BE ASKED

In *Marketing Your Service Business*, Withers & Vipperman say, "Don't wait to be asked. Come up with an interesting topic . . . look up clubs, organizations, and professional associations. Identify those whose membership might include prospective clients, and call the program directors of those organizations."

One key question to answer for yourself is, "Where is your ideal client hanging out?" If you're asked to speak at a meeting where the audience is not your target market, you may be getting exposure, but you may not walk away with any viable prospects.

For most entrepreneurs, a good first place to start would be with your local Chamber of Commerce. Many chambers offer free monthly meetings to their membership where a professional comes in and speaks on a specific topic of interest.

When I started my business in 1989, I got very involved with the Boulder Chamber of Commerce. I presented at what the Chamber called "Brown Bag Lunches," speaking on topics such as:

- "AIDA: A Formula for Successful Copywriting"
- "Surefire Steps for Writing Effective Print Promotions"
- "Direct Is Not a Four-Letter Word"
- And more

Other organizations such as local chapters of the Small Business Development Center, Sales Professionals, Business Marketing Association (BMA) or Business and Professional Women (BPW) are interested in finding new speakers to present to their members as well. That person could be you.

When I moved to Kaua`i, I contacted and ended up delivering presentations for members of the Kaua`i Chamber of Commerce as well as the Kaua`i Small Business Development Center.

There are many options in your local or business community, including, but not limited to:

- Chamber of Commerce
- Small Business Development Center
- Women's business groups (i.e., National Association of Women Business Owners, Business and Professional Women)
- Local business associations
- Meetup groups
- Trade organizations (i.e., International Association of Business Communicators, International Coaching Federation, etc.)
- Fundraising organizations
- Lion's Club
- Zonta International
- Kiwanis Club
- Optimists Club
- Local retirement homes
- Local schools

Many of these organizations are happy to invite you to speak for free. If you'd like to earn an income as a speaker, best to pursue speaking engagements through meeting/event/conference planners. Again, keep your target audience in mind. Go online and search Google for "call for speakers," "call for presenters," or "speaker proposals." Add your city or industry to the search and narrow the playing field even more.

HOW DO YOU GRAB THE ATTENTION OF MEETING PLANNERS?

As a speaking coach, Ava Diamond said that one mistake she sees many speaking rookies make is that they contact a meeting planner and boast about how great they are instead of focusing on the target audience and its challenges. It's just like any marketing effort; it is important to do your research and understand your audience, its problems/issues and the solution you can offer.

When you speak with an event or meeting planner, rather than saying, "I'm Jane Doe and I've spoken to numerous organizations, have appeared on TV and radio, etc.," a better (and more successful) approach is: "Hi, I'm Jane Doe and one of the issues I've noticed in the real estate industry is that REALTORS® struggle with how to build and maintain a client base cost-effectively. What I have is a presentation that addresses how they can market themselves, gain exposure for their businesses and become their clients' trusted advocate without breaking the bank."

See the difference? Once you've gained the planner's attention with a topic that provides a solution to her members, then she'll ask you about your expertise. And at that time, you can fill her in on your background, achievements and experience as a successful speaker. In the example above, if I were Jane Doe, I could then convey my credentials to the meeting planner, which include having been an active REALTOR on the island of Kaua`i as well as having spoken for several REALTOR associations in Hawai`i and Colorado.

INVITE PEOPLE TO YOUR SPEAKING ENGAGEMENTS

Here is a great opportunity to build client relationships and encourage enhanced relationships with prospects without using a hard-sell approach.

When possible, invite clients, colleagues, prospects and friends to your speaking engagements. By hearing you speak, they get the chance to learn more about you without feeling the pressure of a sales pitch. While you are being of service and sharing your professional knowledge in a relaxed, non-threatening environment, they are observing your expertise, confidence and poise.

AFRAID OF PUBLIC SPEAKING?

"If you're reluctant to speak, do the math," says Ava Diamond. "If you have a one hundred dollar product/program/service and you speak twice a month to an audience of fifty people each time, imagine converting fifteen people in the audience into customers. That's fifteen hundred dollars. If the solution you have to offer is a higher price point, then the earning potential, obviously, is greater. You're leaving money on the table—throwing it away—by not getting out and speaking."

Is that a good enough reason for you to stretch yourself outside of your comfort zone and to start pursuing speaking opportunities? I hope so.

"If I have the belief that I can do it, I shall surely acquire the capacity to do it even if I may not have it at the beginning."

— Mahatma Gandhi

EXERCISE:

Which organizations interest you in your community?
Make a list here:

_____

_____

_____

_____

_____

What topics are you most knowledgeable about?

_____

_____

_____

Which of the above topics do you love speaking about?

_____

Who are you going to contact tomorrow?

_____

_____

_____

_____

CHAPTER 6

Releasing the Teacher Within You

*"A teacher takes a hand,
opens a mind and touches a heart."*

— Anonymous

In the last chapter, we explored the fun experience of connecting with people through public speaking. When you teach, you have the same opportunity to connect with others, but there is a difference between these two marketing methods.

WHAT IS THE DIFFERENCE BETWEEN PUBLIC SPEAKING AND TEACHING?

"Having good speaking skills doesn't necessarily make you a good teacher," wrote Tai Goodwin, founder of Bankable Brilliance. "Speaking is all about sharing ideas, experiences, and stories that ignite people to take action or see things in a new way.

"You may be able to do research and put together a presentation on skydiving, but you can't teach someone about skydiving unless you've practiced it yourself. Even if you've done it once—that doesn't mean you know enough to teach it to someone else. You may be able to tell them what you've done, but you don't have enough practical experience to teach them. Teaching is not just telling people what to do, it's showing them how, explaining why and ensuring that they have the correct knowledge to adapt if needed."

Whether you decide to deliver your own workshops or present through a university's continuing education department or community education program, teaching:

- Conveys your knowledge of a subject.
- Portrays you as the expert.
- Increases your exposure.
- Leads to referrals and new opportunities.

As I suggested in the previous chapter about public speaking, don't wait to be asked. When I had an idea to teach a writing class through the Continuing Education department at the University of Colorado at Boulder, I contacted the department and presented my idea. Then, with that success notch on my belt, I approached the Lifelong Learning adult education program through the Boulder Valley School District.

When I lived on the island of Kaua`i, it was a colleague who contacted me and asked whether I would present the first-ever social media program for the Office of Continuing Education and Training at Kaua`i Community College.

As a result of my networking, I have colleagues who contact me with suggestions and referrals for training opportunities. In addition, I have promoted and presented my own workshops/trainings on Kaua`i, Hawai`i, and in Boulder, Colorado.

BOOSTING YOUR CREDIBILITY AND CLIENTELE

The classes I taught were attended by solopreneurs and small business people seeking answers to their business questions. Looking to me as "the expert," many approached me for assistance on their projects. Or they passed my name along to a colleague because they respected my wisdom. It increased my exposure to my target audience as well as my credibility with it—and it can do the same for you.

When she started her business in 2001, Kimberly Pitts held affordable marketing workshops (i.e., $25.00/person) for entrepreneurial women. "I would strive to have ten women at each workshop. Now to some that was setting my limits ways too low," explained Kimberly. "However, I knew that I had to build my name and credibility so I was willing to start small. Hosting these training workshops allowed people to see my training style, my depth of knowledge and my level of support in helping them build their business."

As time went on, Kimberly's workshops grew and she attracted more clients. Fast forward twelve years, she now holds an annual conference and bi-monthly marketing-focused workshops.

"When I started, my biggest cost was $100 for the room rental," she continued. "I was very active in a number of networking groups so I would advertise in those circles. The key to remember is that people do business with those people they feel understand what they need. Plus, they need to feel like they can trust you. So holding these events accomplished that for me."

Best-selling author and founder of Personal Transition Guidance, LLC, PeggyLee Hanson believes in offering teleclasses as a cost-effective marketing tool. "Nothing builds your list faster than hosting your own webinar, seminar, or teleseminar. Bonus: You get to learn it first and then teach it, making *you* an expert! In addition, conference lines can be accessed at no charge as well," she explained.

"Find a subject you need to learn more about in delivering your service. There are many topics to choose from no matter what your field is: marketing; creating your website; how to sell from the stage; speak your platform. These are offered for free by many entrepreneurs who are breaking into or are already very established in the business."

If you'd like to teach, another option to consider is Udemy. Its mission is to help anyone learn anything online. According to its website, Udemy is the world's online learning marketplace, where more than three million students are taking courses in everything from how to start a career as a virtual assistant to yoga lessons. The average instructor earns $7,000 on Udemy and 96 percent of them make sales. If you're interested in becoming one of Udemy's instructors, you may apply online at www.udemy.com/teach

"Within each of us is a teacher, someone who inspires, listens and reflects—who demonstrates by their very being something from which others can grow. Every moment is a moment to learn and to teach."

— Oprah Winfrey

EXERCISE:

What area of expertise do you feel qualified to teach?

_____

What message would you like to share to inspire others?

_____

Is there a university or adult education program in your area? Write down the names of three places you can contact in your community about teaching opportunities:

1. _____

2_____

3. _____

CHAPTER 7

Engaging and Empowering Prospects with Your Words

"If you have other things in your life—family, friends, good productive day work—these can interact with your writing and the sum will be all the richer."

— David Brin

As you just read, one way to reach your ideal clients is to teach your own workshop or approach a local university and offer to present a program through its Continuing Education department. Another way to get your name out to an even larger pool of prospects is by writing articles for local, trade or business publications.

EXPANDING YOUR REACH TO A BROADER AUDIENCE

In addition to reaching a broader audience, publishing articles conveys your knowledge about a specific subject and enhances your professional reputation. Most publications will also include your photo along with a byline that includes your email, website and/or phone number so that readers may contact you.

"Many publications, especially small papers and trade magazines, are quite receptive toward receiving articles written by industry experts," public relations pro John Shors explained. "Since greater demands are placed on editorial departments during a recession, writers get laid-off like everyone else, editors are more inclined to take a close look at what amounts to free content."

In their article "In Search of Ink," Amy and Robert Bly explain, "Just one article in a trade journal can bring a company hundreds of leads and thousands of dollars in sales. And with more than 6,000 magazines from which to choose, it's a safe bet there's at least one that could accommodate a story from your company."

WHO CAN YOU WRITE FOR?

"From *The New York Times*, to ABC News, to HuffingtonPost.com and everyone in between, nearly 30,000 members of the media have quoted HARO sources in their stories. Everyone's an expert at something. Sharing your expertise may land you that big media opportunity you've been looking for." This quote appears on the website for Helpareporter.com (HARO). You can sign up and serve as either one of its sources of information or as a reporter.

HARO sources receive three emails a day with queries from reporters and media outlets worldwide. Scan the emails, and if you're knowledgeable about any of the topics, answer the reporter directly through the anonymous @helpareporter.net email address provided at the beginning of the query.

I responded to a reporter's query when she was seeking information about LinkedIn. Since I speak and consult on this topic, I provided my input and the result was an article she published on American Express' Small Business Open Forum. I received several inquiries from people who found me via her post online.

Another resource to consider is *Writer's Market.* Known as "the most trusted guide to getting published," it outlines thousands of publishing opportunities for writers, including listings for consumer and trade magazines. These listings include contact and submission information to help you get your work published.

In *Marketing Your Consulting and Professional Services*, Connor and Davidson count the number of general, industrial, business, professional and in-house publications, saying, "By using Ulrich's International Periodicals Directory, Bacon's Publicity Checker . . . Standard Periodicals Directory, or Gebbie's All in One Directory, you can obtain the name, address, telephone number, editorial content, fees paid, circulation, target audience, and submission requirements for over 18,000 journal magazines!"

They continue, "There are also over 12,000 newsletters in the United States today, with thousands more worldwide . . . . The Newsletter Yearbook or the Oxbridge Directory of Newsletters are particularly useful. Publication within newsletters may yield the same actual benefits as can be achieved through publication in the larger trade magazines."

Over the years I've written several articles for local business papers such as *The Denver Business Journal, The Kaua`i Business Report, The Advertising & Marketing Review* and the *Boulder County Business Report*, national publications such as *Direct Marketing IQ, DM News, iMarketingNews* and *Direct Marketing* magazine; an international one titled *Direkt* in Germany; online publications such as *Wealth Palace*,

The Review, Work from Home; and several newsletters. I've received phone calls from prospects almost every time. And I discovered that people even saved the articles for future reference—calling me when they needed assistance several weeks, months, or sometimes, even a year later.

In an interview for *The Barefoot Writer*, fellow copywriter Don Hauptman said, "I never cold called. When prospective clients contacted me, I always asked: 'How did you find me?' The answer: 'I read your article' or 'I heard you speak.' And sometimes: 'I read your article and <u>then</u> I heard you speak.'"

SEND COPIES OF YOUR LATEST ARTICLE TO CLIENTS AND PROSPECTS

Maintain a presence while increasing awareness of your services in the marketplace. Simply sending a copy of your latest article (or emailing a link to a website where it's posted) keeps your name in front of clients and prospects. And if you have written a "how-to" article, you also are providing them with complimentary information that's beneficial to them—material that helps them with their future efforts.

Without pitching a sale, you keep them up-to-date on what you are doing, enhance your image and continue to build your credibility in their eyes. This all contributes to developing the KLT Factor (know, like and trust).

SUBMIT TO ARTICLE DIRECTORIES

Another option to broaden your reach is submitting your articles to directories such as EzineArticles.com or GoArticles.com. Search "article submission directories" online and you'll find many more resources.

However, one thing to keep in mind is that some of them prefer original, non-duplicated content. Therefore, it's best not to submit the same article to different directories.

To write original content quickly, freelance writer Brian Scott said, "I set aside a certain amount of time each week to devote myself to writing articles for article submissions. Because my purpose for most of these article directories is to build back links, I don't invest more than 20 minutes to write a single article. I write from my own experience and knowledge so I don't waste time in the research process. I keep each article in the range of 500-550 words in length, nothing over."

Pick up a pen or sit down at your keyboard and start writing your next story.

"I have been successful probably because I have always realized that I knew nothing about writing and have merely tried to tell an interesting story entertainingly."

— Edgar Rice Burroughs

EXERCISE:

Do you blog? What topics have you blogged about that you can turn into articles?

_____

_____

_____

_____

_____

_____

_____

Write down the names of business publications in your community. Find out the name of the editor and contact him/her.

_____

_____

_____

_____

_____

_____

_____

Which industry publications have readers who fit your ideal client profile? Write them down and contact them.

_____

_____

_____

_____

_____

_____

_____

_____

_____

CHAPTER 8

Obtaining Amazing Free Publicity

*"The caterpillar does all the work but
the butterfly gets all the publicity."*

— George Carlin

Millionaire Marketing is about gaining exposure for your business cost-effectively. We've just explored public speaking and teaching, which are great ways to get your message out there. But don't forget to announce your speaking and/or teaching engagements to your community.

GET YOUR MESSAGE OUT THERE WITH PRESS RELEASES

You have just launched a new product nationwide, been acknowledged by a national organization for outstanding achievement in your field or opened an innovative retail store. You want your peers, colleagues, customers and prospects to know about it, but how do you spread your message most effectively? Consider submitting a press release.

First, what's your goal for submitting it? Do you want coverage in a local weekly or monthly business publication, or are you seeking an article in a major nationwide magazine/newspaper?

As former magazine editor Art Spikol explained, "It's easy to send out a lot of releases and get some exposure, and it may work in neighborhood weeklies—but won't work in the major leagues of journalism."

"If you believe you have something that's worthy of, or even requires, public attention, the first thing to do is call us (editors) and explain what you have—a success story, a program, whatever."

Spikol continued to describe his experience as Vice President handling public relations for a large medical center, "We picked up the phone . . . . The result: We got less exposure of the one-column inch variety, and more the feature-story variety."

Calling on editors and establishing a rapport is a very important aspect of public relations. In some cases, even after the phone call, they may request a press release. So, in either case, it is vital for you to know the style and format for writing effective ones.

In this chapter, I'm going to discuss writing press releases that you're submitting to an editor of a publication (either in print or online). However, you may also submit press releases to services online such as PRWeb, PRLog, and WebWire.

STAND OUT FROM THE CROWD

Keep in mind that sending out a press release does NOT guarantee that you will receive coverage. Yours won't be the only press release that an editor receives so you have to "stand out from the crowd."

Former editor for *The Denver Business Journal*, Linda Plofsky

Schneider explained that her experience "shows that they (press releases) fall into one of three categories: the good, the bad and the ugly."

She defined "the good" as those that "contain what is known in journalistic circles as the 'five Ws and the H'—who, what, when, where, why and how. They are provocative, plant seeds of interest about their subject matter and leave the reader wanting more information."

When I started my business in 1989, I began submitting press releases to the business sections of various local (and sometimes trade) papers every time I:

- "Landed" a new account.
- Completed a project for a well-known client.
- Was invited to speak on a topic.
- Received an award.

After several months of doing so, colleagues and peers began commenting, "I always see your name in the paper. Who is doing your marketing?" They were still saying this six months later when my name had not appeared anywhere. Colleagues and prospects connected my name with my face, resulting in increased recognition throughout the local business community.

DO YOU HAVE A FACE FOR RADIO?

In addition to coverage in print media, colleague and business coach Stephanie L.H. Calahan contacts and receives free publicity on Blog Talk Radio shows, podcasts and Google Hangouts on Air (HOA). She has landed many of these speaking engagements by subscribing to a free service known as radioguestlist.com, touted as the number one radio guest, podcast and talk show guest expert interview booking service. When you join its email list, it will send you the latest radio and podcast publicity interview opportunities on a daily basis.

"When I respond to these, knowing that these folks are busy, I keep my query short and sweet, outlining who I serve and the topics I speak on. I've had several people respond and express interest in having me as a guest on their show," explained Stephanie. "I have found that many of the people who listen, reach out to me, opt in for my newsletter, get in my stream and—at some point—they become a client.

"Once I've completed an interview, I ask the host if he/she has any colleagues who are hosting other shows where I should speak. And, believing in reciprocity, I also inquire about whether they would like me to introduce them to any of my colleagues so that they might be guests on their shows as well."

LANDING A COVER STORY IN *USA TODAY*

PR Leads was founded in 2001 as a service to help authors, experts and speakers get the publicity they deserve at a price they could afford.

Their website at prleads.com states that, "More than 3,000 clients who are thought leaders have seen their quotes appear in nearly every major, influential newspaper and magazine as a result of working with them. Publications include the *New York Times, Forbes, Ladies Home Journal, O*, and many B2B publications and leading websites."

When international best-selling author Patrick Snow subscribed to PR Leads in 2002, little did he know that it would result in a cover story in *USA Today*.

In the late summer of 2002, he responded to an inquiry from journalist Stephanie Armour. "When responding to inquiries in the past, I had struck out thirty-three times. However, thirty-four was the 'charmer,'" said Patrick.

"A day after I responded to Stephanie, she emailed me and suggested I call her if I had time. Of course, I had the time and promptly reached out to her. We spoke for about twenty minutes in October. On December 5, 2002, there was my family's photo on the cover of *USA Today*. There was another photo inside the publication on page two as well as on its website. Each was a different photo so there I was (and my book) in *USA Today* three times! And since the paper is owned by the Gannett Company, two weeks later I discovered that the article was the cover feature in the business section of both *The Denver Post* and *Chicago Sun Times*."

That one lead not only resulted in several articles and book sales, it strengthened Patrick's credentials and credibility, which allowed him to increase his speaking fees. And now he has added authority by including a line in his marketing materials that says "As seen in *USA Today*" or "What *USA Today* says about Patrick Snow."

"Many people assume that they need a publicist, but the best publicity is the publicity we do ourselves," Patrick continued.

Wouldn't you like to find yourself on the cover of *USA Today* or another leading publication? You can if you put your mind to it and don't give up. Never say never.

SEVEN HELPFUL HINTS FOR WRITING PRESS RELEASES

In an editor's email inbox or his/her pile of "snail" mail, how do you make *your* press release shout out and say "read me"?

Following these helpful hints may result in receiving some media coverage—the amount of interest generated depends on how and what you write, and whom you target it to.

1. Use a standard press release format.

1a. Use your company's letterhead. At the top of the page, you should always include the following:

Today's date   CONTACT: Name

FOR IMMEDIATE RELEASE   Contact's phone number & email

1b. Always give a contact name. And be sure that the person given as the "contact" knows that he/she has been delegated as such. "This should be someone who is fully informed about every aspect of your product or service and who will drop everything to get the editors what they need for their story angle," explained Teri Lammers, former staff writer for *Inc.* magazine.

There's nothing worse than catching the interest of an editor, having him/her call your contact, and your contact knows nothing about the press release or the subject at hand. How embarrassing!

1c. Always double-space a story so an editor can make comments/changes.

1d. Whenever possible, keep your press release to one page (8½" x 11"). In his book *Practical Publicity: How to Boost Any Cause*, David Tedone reminds his readers that ". . . you are only trying to capture the attention of the editor or reporter, not tell the story in full detail."

Teri Lammers suggested that you "Keep releases to a maximum of two pages—that should present enough information for a short article or generate enough curiosity to get your phone ringing." If your release runs longer than one page, be sure to end the first page with (more) and the last page with # # #.

Remember, the pointers provided in this chapter are guidelines that have been used successfully by professionals. They are to be used as general guidelines to help you. With few exceptions, they are not steadfast rules that have to be followed.

For example, former magazine editor and co-owner of Metzger Albee Public Relations, John Metzger, talked about a semiconductor company that "sent out 'birth announcements' instead of the traditional news release when announcing a new family of products. This unusual approach drew inquiries from editors of seven key trade publications and led to as many articles."

In "Writing Press Releases That Get Results," Sandra Beckwith described a couple in Illinois who sent out a two-page press release regarding their new product. "The two-page release and photo were sent to lifestyle editors at 250 newspapers; 75 used it, generating 3,000 mail orders."

Don't be afraid to experiment. However, if you use a "gimmick," be sure that it is appropriate for the subject matter you're discussing.

2. Keep it simple and straightforward.

2a. Get to the point. Provide significant names, dates, times, places. I try to keep each paragraph to a maximum of six lines. This makes the release look more inviting to the reader's eyes and, in my opinion, is easier to read.

Public Relations Director Christel Beard and Corporate Communications Manager H.J. Dalton, Jr. say, "Make your news release easy to read—and use . . . . Use a short punchy headline . . . . Keep your lead crisp and concise.

"Avoid mind-fogging jargon . . . . They (reporters) need facts laid out clearly, concisely, and in an orderly fashion. They don't need unfamiliar acronyms, jargon, or technical talk; they need to know what's significant and what isn't."

2b. Stick to the facts. Every presentation by an editor that I've heard as well as books or articles I've read on the topic of press releases gives the same advice. Tell the truth. Don't assume anything. From minor details to major ones, make sure the information you provide is accurate.

For example, if you mention "Monday, January 25, 2014," double-check that January 25th does indeed fall on a Monday. Make sure all names are spelled correctly . . . phone numbers are correct, etc.

2c. Personalize your email. When submitting your press release to an editor via email, write a short, snappy and to the point message. *USA Today* columnist Steve Strauss says that when he receives press releases, he looks for "an email that says something like 'Steve, I love your *Ask an Expert* column and think your readers would love to know about the latest twist in finding followers on Twitter . . .'

"1) A little flattery just might get you somewhere, and 2) the person clearly knows me, my beat, my readers, etc. They are not wasting my time," he continued.

3. Create an attention-getting headline.

In talking about how to write potent copy, ad man David Ogilvy said, "The headline is the most important element in most advertisements. It is the telegram which decides whether the reader will read the copy." I believe that this applies to press releases as well.

Remember, yours is one of many press releases coming through an editor's inbox or across his or her desk. In only a few seconds, you have to grab that person's attention and get him or her to read on about your product, service, company, etc.

Here are some of Ogilvy's tips for writing headlines that you can apply toward developing creative press releases that catch the interest of an editor:

- ". . . appeal to the reader's self-interest. It should promise her a benefit, as in my headline for Helena Rubinstein . . . How women over 35 can look younger."

- "Always try to inject news into your headlines, because the consumer is always on the lookout for new products, or new ways to use an old product, or new improvements in an old product."

- "The two most powerful words you can use in a headline are FREE and NEW."

- "Other words and phrases which work wonders are how to, suddenly, now, announcing, introducing, it's here, just arrived, important development, improvement…"

- "People are more likely to read your body copy if your headline arouses their curiosity; so you should end your headline with a lure to read on.

- "Avoid blind headlines—the kind which mean nothing unless you read the body copy underneath them; most people don't."

For more information about writing headlines, turn to Chapter 18.

4. Don't bury the lead.

From one authority to the next, the message is the same—"Don't bury the lead." Here is the advice that three different authors give in their books:

"You must present the essentials immediately and as briefly as possible." — Art Stevens, *The Persuasion Explosion*

"When you sit down to write a news release, make sure you have the answer to these six questions (Who? What? When? Where? Why? or How?) and then write your first paragraph, making sure it contains all this information. . . Why? Many times this is all that will get published of the news release." — Rolf Gompertz, *Publicity Advice & How-To Handbook*

". . . the editor should get the most important news first." — David Tedone, *Practical Publicity*

See what I mean? Most public relations professionals agree, when writing your press release, it is essential that the gist of your story be present in the first paragraph of your release. If you bury what is known in journalism as "the lead" down in your third or fourth paragraph, you risk losing your editor's attention.

To catch the attention of editors immediately, give them your big news first. As Teri Lammers suggested, ". . . important, useful information you should deliver right up front." For example, if you are introducing a new product you can explain how easy it is to use . . . how profitable it is for retailers who will sell it . . . how (if applicable) it ties into any current news or community events . . . etc.

As Beard and Dalton put it, ". . . search hard for a fresh angle that will give your story the proper appeal or 'spin.' This can be done by focusing on things like market share data, price comparisons, an outstanding statistic, or other numbers that play up the uniqueness, size, or quality of your company or product(s) . . . ."

In her article, Sandra Beckwith wrote that, "One business owner capitalized on car-seat legislation. Her release stressed her car-mirror product as a safety device. The release generated 3,000 orders."

Wouldn't you like to generate results like that?

5. Target your market.

In the field of direct marketing, you may have great content, but if you send your message to the wrong audience, you won't get your desired results. The same holds true for submitting press releases.

"Many business owners make the mistake of thinking that a press release is an effective way to flood the market with news about their company. But as with any sales effort, it's a waste of time, energy and money to try to appeal to prospects who have no need for your product or service," explains Beckwith.

She went on to describe a Phoenix-based public relations firm that promoted a company marketing biplane rides:

". . . used her local media database to distribute a feature-oriented release to people with the right titles . . . . Her telephone soon began to ring with requests for interviews . . . . And, it generated more than 30 calls per day from people interested in riding the biplane—a boon for the start-up company, which charged $250 per ride.

"The release worked because it matched a story idea with feature writers and reporters who were interested in pursuing stories about unusual new companies . . . paid advertising in those publications would have cost more than $20,000."

There are no guarantees, but there is also no reason why this can't happen to you. Remember to research the publications you have in mind. "As any savvy marketer will tell you, you don't focus on a particular industry without first doing some in-depth research," claimed Beard and Dalton.

If you've just won an outstanding achievement award, then sending out a release to local weekly or monthly business publications may be enough. If you have just launched a new software product that's a big time and money-saver, then computer and high-tech publications are more likely to bring you better results.

In each case, call the publication first and find out who the appropriate person is for you to contact. Many times you can also go to the publication's website to get the contact information you need.

Consider creating several versions of your release to target specific publications. Simply change your headline or lead-in paragraph so it's appropriate for each market. As Katie Muldoon suggested, ". . . a health story regarding new heart-disease information can have different lead titles—but the same essential information—to attract the editors of men's, women's, health magazines and even general print media."

6. Send out your release in a timely fashion so that it reaches its destination *before* it's old news.

There's nothing worse than announcing a free seminar you are presenting on the 10th of February, but your press release doesn't hit the editor's desk until the 11th. Be sure you plan your public relations efforts with care.

Remember, editors have deadlines too. Keep a list of media deadlines on file so you know exactly when materials need to be in their hands. You might even call before sending out your release to ask how the publication prefers to receive your information.

7. Follow-up, follow-up, follow-up.

Once you have sent your release, take time to follow-up with a telephone call or brief email message. Not only does it help enhance your credibility and establish a rapport, but it gives you the opportunity to provide any information the editor might need to embellish your story.

Sandra Beckwith explained that, "In my career as a publicist, I've found that one effective follow-up strategy is to call an editor to ask if you can answer any questions about the release, or to see if you can provide additional information . . . .

"Another strategy," she continued, "is to tell editors that the release you sent has information they can use in a particular section of their publication." For example, a new restaurant may suggest coverage in the entertainment section. Or a REALTOR® may propose a piece in the real estate section.

When I moved back to Colorado, after living on Kaua`i for ten years, I submitted announcements to two local business publications. After following up with each editor, the result was an article in one publication that focused on five questions about my return to Boulder from Kaua`i. The second publication, while it didn't publish a story about me, ran two articles written by me. I am convinced that, in both circumstances, had I not followed up, I wouldn't have received the exposure.

Steve Strauss (aka Mr. AllBiz) says this about follow up. "We are all busy these days, and things do fall through the cracks. A gentle reminder, a joke, a follow up email, all can be important."

A WORD ABOUT PHOTOS

Personally, having my photo in the paper along with my news increased my visibility in the local business community. However, sending a photo along with your press release doesn't guarantee that it will be printed in a publication. I have found that many times, if space allows, it is included.

Tedone believes that, "A high-quality photo of your subject or speaker is an excellent attention-getting device . . . . Photos work particularly well with short press releases . . . . When editors receive such an announcement with a photo, they will often print the photo and include the who, what, where and so on, as a caption."

In the early to mid-nineties, I used to send a 5" x 7" black and white photo backed with cardboard. On the reverse side of the photo, I requested that it be returned and provided my address. Some publications tell you beforehand that your photograph won't be returned. Others request a self-addressed stamped envelope. And still others return it simply if you request it and supply your address.

Of course, with advanced technology, sending a high-resolution photo via email may be preferred. It's quicker and easier than sending it via "snail" mail and it saves the editor time because he/she won't have to scan it.

Whether you include a photo or not, your success in receiving press coverage comes down to your ability to write clear and concise attention-getting press releases. You don't have to tell an editor your life history, just the vital details that will quickly pique his/her interest.

Remember these three keys to PR success:

1. Get to the point promptly.
2. Stick to the facts.
3. Keep it simple.

I hope to be reading about you soon. Here's to your writing success.

"Publicity is absolutely critical.
A good PR story is infinitely more effective than a front page ad."

— Richard Branson

EXERCISE:

What have you achieved recently that deserves recognition?

_____

_____

_____

_____

_____

What headline could you use to catch attention?

_____

_____

_____

_____

Write down the names of two publications in your local community you can send your press releases to.

1. _____

2. _____

What industry are you in?

_____

Write down the names of three trade publications you can contact.

1. _____

2. _____

3. _____

CHAPTER 9

Tapping into the Power of Partnerships

"One of the most sensible and effective ways to save money marketing is to make allies of other companies and groups reaching out to your target market. Share marketing activities and materials with them."

— Jay Conrad Levinson

Not only is there power in collaborating with your colleagues; there is pleasure. What could be better than connecting in a way that helps both your business and theirs? Joint venture partnerships:

- Increase your exposure to prospects who fit your customer profile.
- Save you time and money, while making you money.
- Provide you with greater visibility and heightened awareness without having to pay the full tab (or sometimes, anything) for such benefits.

For instance, offer to include a flyer for a related business (one that complements your business, not competes with it) in your next customer mailing—in return, your joint venture partners do the same for you.

CREATING ALLIES WITH COLLEAGUES IN RELATED BUSINESSES

In Aspen, Colorado, three booster organizations pooled their resources to create a seven million dollar marketing budget for the ski resort town. The Aspen Chamber Resort Association, Stay Aspen Snowmass and Aspen Skiing Company worked together on some joint efforts as well as coordinated their individual campaigns.

In an article titled, "Better Together," Peter Frett said, "It's about stretching your business opportunities through strategic alliances."

Joint ventures and partnerships are two of the key affordable strategies blogging authority Michelle Shaeffer has used in marketing and growing her business. "What I love most about creating promotions, events, training and products with colleagues and friends is that it allows me to build in accountability, share the workload, and expand my own reach to new audiences," explained Michelle.

"It also helps with the isolation that can happen when one works from home. It's so much more fun and engaging to have someone to brainstorm and get creative with." Some of the joint ventures she has participated in included partnering with colleagues to:

- Present list-building promotions (like the Ultimate Blog Challenge and holiday-themed giveaways).
- Host them on webinars presented to her subscriber list (and they reciprocated the favor, hosting Michelle on their webinars in return).

- Create trainings and workshops where her skills were complementary with theirs, and therefore, together they made a better team and were able to deliver better value than either of them could have accomplished on their own.
- And more.

When you are partnering with a colleague, it's important that you both have values that are in alignment with one another. In other words, is what you have to offer a good fit for the other person's audience (and vice versa)? Are your goals, message and business approach/philosophy in alignment with theirs (and vice versa)?

You each want to bring value to the table not only for one another, but for your customers and clients as well.

Coach and facilitator Adela Rubio has hosted numerous virtual events and more than 200 partnerships. She says, "Partnering helped me grow a really big list and make loads of money. But, I'll be honest with you; that has not been the biggest gift of partnering. The biggest gift from partnering has been the relationships I created—people who started off as joint venture partners and we've actually become dear friends."

THREE WAYS YOU CAN JOINT VENTURE

In her webinar called "Instant Clients Formula," Milana Leshinsky, co-founder of the JV Insider Circle, said joint ventures are the best strategy for getting more clients, selling more products and building a massive email list. Two people combining their energies to cross-promote one another is one of the least expensive ways to get your message out there to your audience.

Wondering what you can do? Similar to Michelle Shaeffer's suggestions, Milana suggests three ways you can joint venture:

1. Teach a class. I have partnered with Michelle where she has hosted me on a teleclass and I taught a five-step copywriting formula. In return, I hosted her on a call where she revealed tips about blogging.

2. Share valuable content. Reciprocate blog posts with one another. The SociaLight Deb Krier has been a guest on my blog, and in exchange, I've posted on her blog. You can recommend colleagues' videos to your subscribers. Your subscribers like it because you're sharing information that helps them and your colleagues who created the videos like it because they're getting "new eyeballs" to their channel.

3. Co-create something together. It can be a book, product, coaching program or an event. Before writing this book, I was a co-author with *New York Times* best-selling author Joel Comm and several colleagues in *So What Do You Do? Discovering the Genius Next Door With One Simple Question.*

After interviewing me for one of her podcasts, Kelly Galea turned the transcript of the interview into an eBook. I did the same after Michelle Shaeffer hosted me on a teleseminar (both can be found on my author page on www.amazon.com/author/debrajason).

If you are concerned that you don't have a large list, keep in mind that a list is just one piece of value. Instead, you may bring time, technical or marketing expertise to the table.

Terry Dean, The Internet Lifestyle Mentor, gave this advice about joint ventures on a guest blog posted on Milana's site, "Don't commit to doing a reciprocal promotion for everyone you contact. Instead figure out what you can do for them. Perhaps it's not a mailing. Maybe you have some other skill you can offer . . . or content you can create exclusively for them . . . or an introduction you can make for them with another expert.

"In a joint venture, everyone wins . . . but the best partnerships happen when different benefits are brought to the table from each partner."

EXERCISE:

What content, skills or expertise do you have?

_____

What values are important to you that you would seek in a joint venture partner?

_____

Make a list of the experts and businesses who currently work with a target market similar to yours.

_____

What relationships do you have that others might find helpful?

_____

CHAPTER 10

Increasing Your Visibility with Social Media

"Social media will help you build up loyalty of your current customers to the point that they will willingly, and for free, tell others about you."

— Bonne Sainsbury

Every time I present *Millionaire Marketing on a Shoestring Budget* as a live workshop, when we start exploring social media marketing, everyone is curious and asks loads of questions. When I ask the question "Are you baffled by social media?" a majority of hands go up.

The topic could be a full-day session on its own, so during these presentations, what I share is what I believe will be of most value to the audience. And that's what I'll reveal to you in this chapter.

SIX LEADING BENEFITS OF SOCIAL MEDIA MARKETING

Before plunging into the world of social media marketing, it is important to determine what your goal is. Why are you diving in? Below you'll find the six top benefits of social media marketing as reported in Social Media Examiner's "2014 Social Media Marketing Industry

Report" by Michael Stelzner:

1. Generating exposure for your business (92 percent up from 89 percent in 2013).

- With as little as six hours per week, 95 percent of those conducting social media activities indicated that it generated exposure for their business.
- Nearly all marketers (93 percent) who have been using social media marketing for a year or longer report that it generates exposure for their biz.

2. Increasing traffic (80 percent up from 75 percent in 2013).

- 84 percent of marketers found that increased traffic occurred with as little as six hours per week invested in social media.
- Those who have used social media for one year or more reported substantially better results (79 percent) compared to those with less experience.

3. Developing loyal fans (72 percent up from 65 percent in 2013).

- 77 percent of B2C companies were more likely to develop a loyal fan base through social media than B2B marketers (64 percent).
- Of those using social media for at least a year, 69 percent found it useful for building a loyal fan base.

4. Providing market place insight (71 percent up from 69 percent in 2013).

- At least 74 percent of those spending six hours per week were more likely to gain marketplace insight.
- Of those with at least one year of experience, 69 percent or more found social platforms provided marketplace insight.

5. Generating leads (66 percent up from 61 percent in 2013).

- By spending as little as six hours per week, 66 percent of marketers saw lead generation benefits with social media.
- More than half of marketers with at least one year of social media experience were generating leads with social platforms.

6. Improving search engine rankings (61 percent up from 58 percent in 2013).

- At least 60 percent of those investing six hours per week in social media marketing saw improvements in search engine rankings.
- 58 percent of those businesses using social media for one year or longer reported a rise in their search engine rankings.

Though it was second to last on the list of benefits, since this book is about cost-effective marketing tools, I thought it important to mention that *51 percent (up from 47 percent in 2013) of businesses said that implementing social media efforts reduced their marketing expenses.*

Nearly half who spent six hours a week on social media efforts saw the benefit of reduced marketing expenses. At least 57 percent of businesses with ten or fewer employees agreed that social media marketing reduced marketing expenses.

SOCIAL MEDIA: IT'S MORE THAN YOU THINK

During my presentations on the topic of social media marketing, I ask the attendees whether they use social media marketing as a tool. For those who say, "Yes," I then follow up by asking what they are doing. The replies are usually, "Facebook, Twitter, LinkedIn." Think about it. When you're having a conversation and you say "social media," most people have Facebook on their minds. Don't they?

Well, social media is much more than Facebook, Twitter, and LinkedIn. The aforementioned statistics refer to a variety of social media marketing tools that include:

- *Blogging* – more than 210 million blogs online and growing.
- *Submitting articles* – ezinearticles.com, examiner.com, articlealley.com, GoArticles.com
- *Bookmarks* – delicious.com, digg.com, stumbleupon.com, reddit.com
- *Press release submission* – prnewswire.com, prweb.com, free-press-release.com, PRLog.org
- *Photo and Video Sharing* – instragram.com, youtube.com, vimeo.com, flickr.com
- *And of course, last but not least . . .*

THE SITES YOU'VE ALL HEARD ABOUT – SOCIAL NETWORKING

- Facebook – If Facebook were a country, it would be the world's third largest (as of the first quarter of 2014, more than one billion users).

- Twitter – September 2013, over one billion registered users (255 million active users).
- LinkedIn – The world's largest professional network on the Internet with more than 330 million members in over 200 countries and territories. (More than one million are small business owners.)
- Pinterest – There are more than thirty million "pins" on Pinterest. Pinterest doesn't make its numbers public, but in February 2013, Reuters & ComScore stated that Pinterest had 48.7 million users.
- Google Plus – A *New York Times* article posted in February 2014 reported that Google says Google Plus has 540 million monthly active users.

It is my guess that, by the time you read this book, these numbers will have all increased substantially.

INTERESTING SOCIAL MEDIA STATISTICS TO CONSIDER

If you are a reader who has been hesitant to plunge into the world of social media, keep this in mind:

- In 2014, 92 percent of marketers said social media was important to their businesses (up from 86 percent in 2013).
- Social media has become the #1 activity on the Web.
- Facebook, Twitter, LinkedIn, YouTube and blogging are the top five social media tools being used by marketers (Facebook leads the pack with 94 percent).

WHAT DOES SOCIAL MEDIA MEAN TO YOU?

Colleague Ellen Britt, founder of Pink Coattails, wrote a blog post titled "Take Off Your Social Media Mask On Facebook And Be Yourself."

In it, she said, "Your customers and clients and even your potential customers and clients are not on social media to get their problems solved. And they are definitely not there to buy stuff. They just want to . . . well . . . *socialize.*

"This includes looking at and sharing pictures of cute cats and fabulous food and videos of three-legged dogs and even strange people wearing funny hats as well as catching up with what's going on with their friends and family members."

Where many marketers "miss the mark" is thinking social media is all about selling.

"That's not to say they'll [your customers/clients] never purchase something on social media, it's just that this is not top of mind for them," Ellen continued.

I loved Ellen's post because it resonates with the message I share when speaking on the topic of social media (and marketing, in general).

Folks, it's all about building relationships—establishing the KLT Factor—*first!*

Jeff Walker, author of *Launch* and creator of Product Launch Formula, says, "We are more influenced by people we like than those we don't like . . . . And the more likeable you are, the more influence you will have . . . . Building trust is the ultimate short circuit to becoming influential in someone's life."

Laura Rubinstein, author of *Social Media Myths Busted*, expresses it this way, "The bottom line about the social media ROI misconception is that social media is not a direct sales tool. Rather, it is a relationship-building platform. When you effectively build relationships, business happens. Thus, if you can build a loyal community of raving fans, you will profit because of your growth in visibility and connectivity on social media."

WHAT IS BEING SOCIAL ANYWAY?

Let's take a look at the word "social." According to *Websters II New Riverside Dictionary*, it means:

1. Living in communities or groups. 2. Of or relating to the life & interrelationships of human beings in society. 3. Marked by friendly companionship with others.

What you do offline, day-to-day, is social. After all, you are:

- Involved in community – Perhaps in your child's school, your neighborhood, your workplace, etc.
- Relating to the life of human beings – Asking "How are you?," or "How are the kids, the family, the dog?" when you are at work or standing in line at the grocery store.
- Establishing friendly companionship – Taking a walk with a friend, meeting for coffee—connecting, building relationships and engaging.

In our technology-based society, social media involves the same thing:

- Interacting in communities.
- Engaging and developing trust.
- Building relationship with others.

Just doing it *online!*

Personally, I have met many people thanks to Facebook, Twitter, LinkedIn, etc.—people I don't think I would have met otherwise.

Many of them are business professionals, and we've met virtually, not because of some pitch I posted, but because of mutual connections. Then we have stayed in touch and developed friendships because we've each been true to, and shared, our authentic selves. And you will find quite a few of them quoted in this book.

As a result of some of these connections, I've been invited to be a guest on webinars, teleseminars, telesummits, and/or Blog Talk Radio shows hosted by people I've met on social media (but may have never met in person).

I am *so* grateful that, in many cases, I have actually met several of these people face-to-face, which has helped me continually develop and build on that KLT Factor you've seen me mention several times throughout this book.

If you're frustrated with social media and struggling to sell on these networks, here is a tip . . . RELAX!

JUST BE YOURSELF

You never know who you may connect with simply by posting that fabulous feline or that cute canine gazing up at you with big brown eyes. Will it convert to a sale? Perhaps, at some point in time. But first it will convert into friendships—personally and professionally—that have the potential to last a lifetime!

Internet pioneer Joel Comm says, "I think you have to develop that know, like and trust before your audience can be leveraged to pay you. So, if you're looking at social media as a 'hey, here's my opportunity to sell my stuff,' then you're going about it the wrong way. Social media is a long term play. You have to build relationships."

And, Erik Qualman, author of *Socialnomics*, reminds us that, "We don't have a choice on whether we do social media, the question is how well we do it."

MAXIMIZING YOUR ONLINE NETWORKING EXPERIENCE

In Chapter 4, we addressed taking a leadership role in your business through face-to-face networking. Here we'll explore the concept of taking traditional offline networking, online.

In an interview with business vision catalyst Stephanie L.H. Calahan, she revealed that participating in social media groups has been an extremely effective marketing strategy.

"However, I do what most people don't do when it comes to these groups. The way most people participate in social media groups is to bombard the group with comments along the lines of, 'Hey, I have this program going on or hey I have this new thing going on.' It's advertising."

Networking CEO Patty Farmer runs a couple of groups on Facebook. "I'm committed to keeping the group focused on service— where we serve each other. Each group is targeted to a specific audience and stresses the value of collaboration. This way it's an effective networking platform for everyone involved."

"I use social media groups to connect with people and actually very rarely do I promote. I hold conversations within each group," Stephanie continued. "Occasionally I might share a link or two to my website if it applies to a conversation that's happening. But, I give—give with the expectation to receive at some point. So, if a person is having a challenge with something, I'm going to share something I feel will help them solve that problem, a great resource for them, or I'll introduce other people who can help them. It's traditional networking done online."

Over time, Stephanie has found that the more she takes this approach to helping people, whether it's in Google Plus communities, LinkedIn groups or Facebook groups, the more they get curious. "Because they start seeing me everywhere. And, they think 'Who is this person? Who is this Stephanie?' Then, they visit my site, look a little closer and they contact me," she continued.

"As a result, people see me in so many different places and have resonated with my responses (and that I wasn't trying to promote all the time). They recognized that I was legitimately and authentically trying to help and that resonated with them."

I share a similar concept when I deliver presentations about LinkedIn. I speak about LinkedIn groups and the significance of getting involved (see Chapter 11). It's important to remember that participating in these groups is not about "I have this to sell and that to sell." It's about sharing information and adding value whether it is your own post or a discussion someone else has posted and you're contributing to the conversation.

I have seen discussions where someone posts a specific question, and before answering the question (and sometimes not even answering it at all), someone will respond with "Call me and I can sell you a widget that will help."

"There are so many people who do it wrong and alienate people," suggested Stephanie. "If you really want people to connect with you, start interacting. Yes, it takes time, but building relationships doesn't happen overnight. They take time."

Stephanie's point is a good reminder worth repeating. Don't rush it. Whether online or off, building relationships takes time. Someone may not call you tomorrow, but when you have nurtured that "know, like and trust," when the time is right, and they need your help in a different way, people will think, "Now is the time, so I'm going to send her a private message and reach out to her."

THE BEST SOCIAL NETWORKER I KNEW —MY GOLDEN RETRIEVER, IKE

In his book *How to Win Friends and Influence People*, Dale Carnegie wrote, "Why not study the technique of the greatest winner of friends the world has ever known? Who is he? You may meet him tomorrow coming down the street. When you get within ten feet of him, he will begin to wag his tail. If you stop and pat him, he will almost jump out of his skin to show you how much he likes you. And, you know that behind this show of affection on his part, there are no ulterior motives . . . ."

When I lived on the island of Kaua`i, I was fortunate to own the world's most awesome dog. A golden retriever, Ike was young at heart till his last dying day (he was 13½ years old). Get him to the beach and he thought he was a puppy. I write about him because I am grateful to have had him in my life, and he was the best social networker I knew. (No, he didn't have his own Facebook page.)

Ike was a total beach dog. His "job" was fetching, and while he never begged for food, he would stand at your feet, look up at you with his big brown eyes and push a stick toward you—repeatedly—until you picked it up. He begged for fetching.

He was persistent, but rarely did anyone deny him his request. Even one of the country's past Presidents couldn't say no to Ike. Rumor had it that the Clintons were on Kaua`i, and I knew, if it were true, that they would be staying nearby at the home of one of my clients. As I strolled the beach with Ike one day, sure enough there they were talking to a friend—and one of Ike's biggest fans—Pierce Brosnan. Pierce introduced us to both President Bill Clinton and Hillary.

I found it humorous that, when introducing Ike to President Clinton, Pierce said, "This is Ike. He's famous." I looked at the former President, smiled, and said, "That sounds funny coming from a former 007 star, don't you think?" As I chatted with Hillary, President Clinton walked off to play with Ike. After throwing and fetching a few sticks along the beach and into the ocean, they returned and President Clinton told me, "I love your dog." Ike loved to swim. He used to dive too!

Wouldn't we all like that? To stand before prospects, look at them with our big blue (brown, green, etc.) eyes and not have to say a word? They would know how we could best serve them?

NETWORKING IS FOR THE DOGS

Networking is not just about going to business events or participating in social media groups. You can do it anywhere—even on the beach with your dog.

In addition to being great at meeting people on his own, I always met people when I walked the beach with Ike. Some of them have become dear friends (and are proud owners of "*I like Ike*" t-shirts). And some of them became business connections. That's why I have repeatedly said he is the best social networker I know.

Ike definitely preferred people to other dogs. That's because he thought he was a person too. I am so lucky to have had him in my life. He was an awesome companion who oozed love and brought smiles to the face of everyone he met. He had a heart of gold.

Do you have a dog? When you're out walking, do you find you meet people everywhere you go when your dog is with you? You may have noticed that there are dogs with their own Facebook profiles (my colleague Brian G. Johnson has one for his standard poodle, Otis)—that's because people love them. Our pets bring us together in more ways than we may realize, both online and off.

"Dogs are not our whole life, but they make our lives whole."

— Roger Caras

EXERCISE:

What does social media mean to you? Fill in your answer below.

_____

_____

_____

_____

_____

What is your goal with social media marketing?

_____

_____

_____

Which social networks are you going to focus on?

_____

_____

_____

_____

How much time do you want to commit to posting on social networks?

_____

_____

_____

What content will you share with others to create engagement?

_____

_____

_____

_____

_____

_____

CHAPTER 11

Leveraging the Lead-Generating Power of Linkedin

*"It's not about closing sales,
it's about opening relationships."*

— Kevin Knebl

Back in 2007, I received an invitation from a friend to join him on his LinkedIn network. His wasn't the first invite I had received. At that time, I hadn't heard about LinkedIn so I ignored not only his request, but all the previous ones I had received as well. However, soon after, I started to receive even more invites from numerous colleagues. Intrigued, I agreed and said, "Sure, let's get LinkedIn."

I didn't give it much thought. I accepted the invitations, but I still wasn't quite clear on the value of this social network and how it would benefit me.

I decided it was time to start asking questions and learning more about this phenomenon. Curious, I contacted a colleague and asked why he liked it and why he thought it was important to jump on the

LinkedIn bandwagon. He said there was value in connecting with others online and starting conversations with others on the network. He had even gotten new business this way. With that feedback, I took a different approach, reworked my profile and started getting more involved.

SOUND FAMILIAR? ARE YOU CONFUSED ABOUT LINKEDIN?

When I speak on the topic of LinkedIn today, many people in the audience will say "A friend invited me so I said 'Yes,' but I don't really know what I'm doing." Are you one of those people?

Patty Kulton with Caliber Home Loans was one of those people. "When I met Debra I knew nothing about LinkedIn. After a one-on-one consultation, I learned the value of fully completing my profile and how to make LinkedIn work for me. With her knowledge I have discovered how LinkedIn will help me grow my business. For those who seek help optimizing their profile and want to make the most of their LinkedIn experience, I highly recommend Debra."

If you are like Patty once was, I want to change that. I want to clear up the confusion so you can leverage the lead-generating power of LinkedIn.

As of this printing, with more than 330 million members (it was 75 million in 2010) in over 200 countries, LinkedIn is the world's largest professional networking site. By interacting with members, via groups and discussions, you give other like-minded colleagues the opportunity to get to know, like and trust you—three vital keys to building successful relationships.

COPYWRITING TIPS TO OPTIMIZE YOUR PROFILE WITH KEYWORDS

Creating your professional profile is more than just posting your resume. Similar to your website, when you're writing content, it's important to utilize keyword phrases in your profile. After all, when prospects are searching for someone like you—which they do on LinkedIn—you want to show up high on their results list.

For instance, a few of the phrases I have used in my headline are "copywriting services," "professional speaker" or "direct response copywriter." So I have these keywords placed throughout in at least six strategic locations of my profile.

SIX PLACES TO INCLUDE YOUR KEYWORDS WHEN SETTING UP YOUR PROFILE

1. Your professional "headline" – This appears right below your name on your profile. Be concise. Use descriptive phrases you think someone might search to find a professional like you. Unless you work for a big-name brand, it's not likely someone will be searching for "President of the ABC Company." Consider using a tag line as well, one that incorporates a keyword phrase. LinkedIn gives you up to 120 characters here.

2. Current work experience – Include the keyword phrase(s) in the title and in the description of the work you do.

3. Past work experience – Weave the keyword phrase(s) in where you can, only if it's appropriate. (This is not about stuffing your keywords everywhere. It needs to make sense.)

4. Skills and endorsements – List the key areas that you specialize in—areas of expertise that you want others to endorse you for. If you find people are endorsing you for skills you don't want to be recognized for, you can edit and delete those from your profile. LinkedIn shows the top ten skills that you're receiving endorsements for on your profile.

When I receive an endorsement for a skill I'd rather not be known for, I follow up with the colleague who was kind enough to endorse me. I don't say "I don't want to be endorsed for that." Instead, I thank the person for the endorsement and let him or her know which skills I'd welcome endorsements for. And I ask which skills he or she would like to be endorsed for. Reciprocity goes a long way.

5. Websites – Under your "Contact Info" tab, you can list up to three website links. Many people just insert one thinking, "I have one website." However, if that's the case, why not take advantage of this opportunity to lead people to several pages of your website?

And while you're listing websites, you may use keyword phrases to describe each link.

Take a look at what you have under "Contact Info" now. Perhaps it says "Personal website," "Blog," or "Company website." Instead, if you were a REALTOR® in Boulder, Colorado, it could say "Boulder Real Estate" or "Boulder County REALTOR." You could then take the person to another page on your site with a keyword phrase such as "Search Boulder real estate." See where I'm heading with this?

Remember, you may submit up to three website links. So if you don't have three websites, simply use this opportunity to direct folks to other pages of the one website you do have. In my profile, viewers have the option to go to the home page of my copywriting site ("Freelance copywriting services" is the keyword phrase), my portfolio page ("Copywriting portfolio samples") or my speaker page ("Marketing seminars").

Do the same on your LinkedIn profile. Optimize your website options for keyword phrases while giving visitors the option to learn more about you on various pages of your site.

Here's a blog post I wrote that outlines the four simple steps to make this change to the website links on your profile: www.writedirection. com/optimize-linkedin-website-links-keyword-phrases

6. Summary – This is the most important section of your profile because it reveals a personal side of yourself and communicates who you are. It also conveys what you're passionate about and how you can help others.

Avoid having really long paragraphs here. Don't make readers dig deep to read your information. Shorter paragraphs make the content more inviting to the readers' eyes. And consider using sub-headings (which can also be keyword enhanced).

LinkedIn allows you to use up to 2,000 characters here so take advantage of the opportunity to express yourself. Write your Summary in first person, and give readers some insight about your personality and your desire to be of service to them.

Whether you're already a LinkedIn member or thinking about it, take advantage of these six strategies when you're writing your profile. They'll help you harness the power of the world's largest professional networking site. It's a place to access valuable information, become part of a conversation and connect with other professionals.

I have generated leads and clients through my LinkedIn profile.

Here's what one had to say:

"When I found Debra on LinkedIn, I was impressed by the initial writing that she had there and by the breadth of writing she had done for companies similar to ours. I was very pleased at how quickly she grasped our business of mobile marketing and how she asked all of the right (write) questions to make it easy on me. In fact, some of her questioning was so in-depth that it helped me refine our own sales pitches. I would highly recommend Debra . . . . She has exceeded my expectations." — Bob Bentz, ATS Mobile (formerly Advanced Telecom Services), King of Prussia, PA

I'm confident that this can happen for you as well.

ARE YOU MAKING THE BIGGEST MISTAKE ON LINKEDIN?

Want to join my LinkedIn network? Visit me at www.linkedin. com/in/debrajason. Send me an invitation, but here's an important tip to keep in mind . . .

The biggest mistake people make when inviting others to LinkedIn is clicking "connect" and using LinkedIn's generic invitation. Remember, this is about building relationships, and the best way to start relationships is with a personalized invitation explaining why you're reaching out.

When you invite someone to connect with you, don't use LinkedIn's generic invitation—especially if you've never met the person (or don't know him or her well enough). This invitation is the beginning of a conversation and the opportunity to build relationships. Take the extra few moments to personalize your invitation and explain who you are and why you'd like to connect.

Another mistake people make is ignoring invitations they receive from people they don't know. Before you decide to ignore those invites, take a moment to view the profile of the person who contacted you. It might be a qualified lead or a person worth connecting with. Here's what I suggest . . .

When you receive the invite, there's an option to "accept" or "reply but don't accept." After viewing the person's profile, here's what I do if I think the person is a worthwhile connection. I hit "reply but don't accept" and send a personalized message asking how the person found me—was he or she referred to me by someone or simply searching LinkedIn?

I explain that it helps me to know how people are connecting with me. If the person doesn't respond, then I don't accept the invite. After all, as I've said, it's about beginning to build a relationship and have a conversation. So if you don't reply to my first attempt to start that conversation, then perhaps you were only trying to add numbers to your contacts versus beginning a mutually beneficial connection.

ARE YOU GETTING INVOLVED ON LINKEDIN?

In Chapter 4, we talked about not just joining, but getting involved in professional organizations. It's not enough just to pay your dues; it's important to become part of the community—attend events, volunteer for committees, serve on a Board of Directors, etc.

It's similar with LinkedIn. Becoming a member of the network, completing your profile and sitting back waiting for people to contact you is not the way to develop powerful relationships.

Pay attention to and participate in LinkedIn groups related to those things that interest you—personally and professionally. To date, there are more than two million groups to choose from, so peruse the site and seek out those that offer you exposure to your ideal clients, referrals and/or resources.

As highlighted in the previous chapter, keep in mind that participating in LinkedIn or any other social networking group is about connecting with others, contributing to the discussion in a productive way that helps others (vs. pitching whatever product, program or service you may represent). The value comes from offering solutions, opinions and/or advice, having conversations and developing relationships. Those connections may eventually lead to *prosperous* relationships.

Check out the discussions happening in those groups that interest you and jump into the conversation when you have something to share on the topic. You'll not only establish authority and credibility with your contributions, but you'll start "meeting" new colleagues virtually and strengthening your network of prospective referral resources, business affiliates and potential clients.

WHAT *NOT* TO DO ON LINKEDIN

I featured this guest post on my blog by my colleague Deb Krier, The SociaLight, about "What NOT To Do On LinkedIn." She explained this scenario as follows:

> When I get a request to connect from someone I don't know, I look at their Profile—especially if they didn't tell me "why" they wanted to connect. Unless it's clear that they are a spammer, I'll connect.

Recently, I received a request to connect from a woman who didn't give me a reason and used the default of "I'd like to add you to my professional network on LinkedIn."

When I viewed her Profile, it appeared that she was fairly new to LinkedIn. She has less than 200 connections and her Profile is extremely sparse. She only has her current (Consultant at Self Employed) and prior job, as well as one listing for education—none of which contained any information or detail.

She also didn't have a Summary or any further information. But, I connected anyway because I often have "newbies" connect with me so they can learn more about LinkedIn.

Within three days, I received this message from her, via LinkedIn:

"Hello,
Did I hear right? Are you guys considering voice over IP?
If so, make sure you read this: [URL]
Good luck".

Not sure where she "heard" I was considering VOIP, as I'm not. I also didn't click the link, for fear it was a virus, spam, or otherwise harmful.

The next day, I received another message:

"Hello,

I recently came across a vendor who has links to social media pro-files! Instead of using lists as we have for years, we changed it up a little and started to do a little more research on the person so we can have more targeted campaigns, this has helped us tremendously! This is definitely a new way to market. If you ever need anything like this, I suggest you contact [name and email address]. She can also help you with any of your other marketing needs."

Huh?

This time, I replied, stating that the power of LinkedIn lies in developing relationships with people, not in spamming them with unsolicited sales messages. I also pointed out that if she had read my Profile, she wouldn't be suggesting I needed to learn about social media!

I'll admit, I may have been a bit snarky, and she never responded.

Deb explained that she had several reasons to write about this:

1. The woman who contacted her had a Profile that was so incomplete that it was doing her more harm than good. Everyone is a "beginner" on LinkedIn at some point—but before really connecting with people, make sure your Profile is very robust and complete.

2. She made a crucial error in sending spammy messages. While Deb didn't report her to LinkedIn, someone else may—and she could lose her account. Maybe it doesn't mean that much to her, but why risk it?

3. As Deb conveyed to her, successfully using LinkedIn is all about developing relationships—not "sell, sell, sell."

Whether you're inviting someone to connect with you on LinkedIn or accepting an invitation, be clear on what your goal is. Unfortunately, it seems there will always be those people who abuse the system. Ignore them and move on to those quality relationships that are available to you.

CUSTOMIZING YOUR LINKEDIN URL

During one of my programs titled, "Unleashing the Lead-Generating Power of LinkedIn," we get online and take a quick peek at some of the participants' LinkedIn profiles. And, nine times out of ten, they're using the lengthy URLs that LinkedIn assigns when they first publish their profiles.

Most often, these people don't even realize that they have the ability to customize their LinkedIn URL. You see, when you sign up for a Profile, LinkedIn assigns you a URL that looks something like this:

www.linkedin.com/pub/your-name/88/892/674

Now, imagine you're in a conversation and someone asks whether she can find you on LinkedIn. Would you even remember the above link? Not likely.

So why not make it easy on yourself and others? LinkedIn lets you do this quickly and easily so you can have a URL that reads www.linkedin.com/in/yourname.

Here are six steps to follow and you'll be done:

1. Go to your LinkedIn Profile and select "Edit Profile."

2. Find the "Contact Info" tab and click on that.

3. Next to your current URL it should say "Edit" (or there may be a blue pencil). After you click on that, you'll see a box that says

"Your public profile URL."

4. In that box, you'll see your Current Profile URL and underneath it you can click on "Customize your public profile URL."

5. A new box will pop up that says "Enhance your personal brand by creating a custom URL for your LinkedIn public profile. If you change your URL, your current custom URL will no longer be valid."

   Below that it will display: www.linkedin.com/in with your name auto-filled in the box next to it. If you want to use your name the way they have it auto-filled, then move to step #6 (below). Otherwise, you can change the name in the box to whatever you want to use.

6. Click the button that says "Set Custom URL." If your name is available, you're good to go. If not, LinkedIn will suggest alternatives or you can enter a new one that you prefer.

That's it. Just six simple steps and you're set. Simply share your easy-to-remember URL and don't forget to incorporate it in all your marketing (i.e., email signatures, business cards, website, etc.)

LINKEDIN ATTENDEES PRAISE DEBRA'S GUIDANCE

"I really enjoyed your LinkedIn presentation. It will assist me in receiving high quality leads and the techniques to communicate with the leads and build relationships, one area that I was lacking . . . . Thanks again for sharing your knowledge." — C. McCoy, Keller Williams, Lone Tree, CO

"I learned more in two hours listening and working with Debra than I have been able to accomplish on my own on LinkedIn in the past 6 months. Thank you again for all of your time and expertise!" — K. Wexler, GENASSIST, Inc., Denver, CO

"Debra gave an in-depth and highly informative presentation on LinkedIn . . . . I came away with more information and understanding about how to make LinkedIn work for my business than ever before! Demonstrating just how to maneuver through LinkedIn right there online was really valuable. Personable and entertaining too. Thanks Debra!" — K. Bielanski, RE/MAX of Boulder, Boulder, CO

"Debra is aware of the level of experience of those she tutors at these sessions—most are unfamiliar—like myself—with social media so she is patient, thorough in responses to queries, and reviews important points of the discussion throughout the presentation. As a student I have become more aware of what LinkedIn can do for my users because of the do's and don'ts when using the site. I now understand the true purpose of building a network of professionals nationwide." — M. Kusaka, RE/MAX Kaua`i, Lihue, HI

"Debra, thank you for taking the time out of your busy schedule to show us how to increase our business revenue. The fast paced social media that we must incorporate in our business is extremely time consuming, however, very critical. Your thoroughness in highlighting the necessary sections and emphasizing the appropriate keywords to help us enhance the lead generation traffic to our site was definitely something I know is useful for me and lacking on my profile." — D. Sales-Luis, Kaua`i Pacific Real Estate, Kapaa, HI

I share the above endorsements with you, not to brag, but to help you realize that if you are questioning why you're on LinkedIn, you can learn how to maximize your experience. If you like connecting with people, LinkedIn provides you with an easier-than-you-think opportunity to do so. Are you taking advantage of the lead-generating power of LinkedIn?

EXERCISE:

What are some of the keyword phrases you should have in your profile? Think about the phrase prospects would use to find someone like you when they don't know your name or business.

_____

_____

_____

_____

_____

Create your professional headline here. Taking the keyword phrases you wrote above, use up to 120 characters to write a headline for your LinkedIn profile.

_____

_____

_____

_____

_____

Think about how you might incorporate some of your keyword phrases into your past job experience. Write down your ideas here.

_____

_____

_____

Write down four interests you have. Then search LinkedIn for groups that you might want to join and get involved in the discussion.

1. _____

2. _____

3. _____

4. _____

CHAPTER 12

Your Ticket to Eliminating the Overwhelming Feeling You Get from Social Media

"Don't sign up for every social media site all at once. Do one or two things well and then add more."

— Andrea Vahl aka Grandma Mary,
Social Media Edutainer

In the last two chapters, we explored increasing your visibility via social media marketing as well as maximizing your LinkedIn experience. I chose to cover LinkedIn because it's the largest social network for business professionals. However, there are many other social networks to participate in—so many that deciding on where to focus your efforts can be confusing and/or overwhelming.

ARE YOU BAFFLED BY SOCIAL MEDIA?

When I speak about social media marketing—or just in

everyday conversation around the topic—two questions that come up repeatedly are:

1) Do I have to do it all? LinkedIn, Twitter, Facebook, Google Plus, Pinterest, Instagram, Klout?

2) It takes so much time, I get overwhelmed. How much time should I spend on it?

While you may read posts or articles about "Social Media in 5 Minutes a Day," I'm not one to make that promise. Social media marketing does require your time and attention. However, here is what I suggest as the ticket to eliminating the overwhelming feeling you get from social media . . .

YOU DON'T HAVE TO DO IT ALL AT ONCE!

I know, I know. You hear you need to be everywhere. You think you may be missing out, missing leads and business opportunities, if you don't do it all. I, too, felt that way, but alas, I came to grips with the fact that I am (and you are) only human. And not super human at that.

Most of my focus is on Facebook, Twitter and LinkedIn. I do have Google Plus, Pinterest and YouTube accounts, but don't spend as much time and energy there. And I've finally come to peace with that.

As I said, you are only human, so give yourself permission to start off gently. Pick one (okay, maybe two) network(s) where you feel most comfortable, where your peeps are hanging out, and where you enjoy spending your time.

"You may be leaving biz on the table," says colleague Joel Comm. "But guess what? There's no way you can do it all. Just keeping up with one network on a regular basis takes time."

The SociaLight, Deb Krier, puts it this way: "Before you even dip your toes into the social media pool, determine which sites you're going to use. It's just like networking in person—it may be fun to see people, but if it doesn't benefit your business, is it a good use of your time? The same goes for social media. Determine which sites will be the most beneficial for your business and spend time there."

You can read Deb's guest post about "Two Tips For Social Media Success in 15 Minutes" on my blog at www.writedirection.com/social-media-success-15-minutes

In his podcast addressing the overwhelming feeling some people get from doing social media, Joel explained that there are two instances in which he uses social media:

1. When he has something to say.
2. When he wants to interact with others.

Simple and sound philosophy, don't you think? He goes on to say, "I'm going to set you free from the burden of social media." How does he do that? Easy . . .

"Be yourself. Do it [social media] in a way that fits with who you are and your lifestyle. Don't guilt yourself because it's a burden you can't carry."

I loved when Joel shared this: "Social media is addictive in nature and it's an insatiable beast that can never be fully fed. There's no way you can do it all . . . . Let social media be an extension of who you are. Isn't that more authentic anyhow?"

"Make peace with the fact that you may lose traffic by not using one network vs. another. You can't be there for friends, fans and followers all the time, because *you have a life*."

"Let those social media shackles fall off. Live your life the way you want to and let social media be the slave to you—not the other way around. You master it . . . . Do whatever works for you. Do it your way." (When Joel said this, in my head I immediately heard Frank Sinatra singing "I did it my way.")

STRESS-RELIEVING, TIME-SAVING SOCIAL MEDIA TOOLS

Tools are available to save you time and relieve you from that overwhelming feeling you may experience from social media.

The one I use, and have been using for years, is Hootsuite (www.hootsuite.com). From one dashboard, you can schedule Facebook posts, Tweets, LinkedIn updates and more. You can also monitor conversations. There are both free and paid plans available to you.

Colleague Deb Krier recommends Buffer (www.bufferapp.com). It is a scheduling program for posting several articles at once, across your social media accounts, with the actual posting times varying. Buffer also offers free as well as paid options.

Deb also suggests setting a timer for fifteen minutes to help you keep focused. "There are lots and lots of fun and interesting things to look at on social media and it's hard not to get sucked in with all the bright, shiny objects. You can always go back when you're not working and catch up."

Are you taking the ticket to eliminating the overwhelming feeling you get from social media?

Social media can be a lot of fun. If it is not feeling that way for you, then take some time to re-evaluate what you are doing. As Deb suggests, social media can suck you in, but you want to stay productive.

If you feel like you're juggling too many balls, then it may be time to set some aside for now. After all, you're in business for yourself because you enjoy the freedom it gives you. So set yourself free from being overwhelmed by social media and take it one step at a time so that it's something you enjoy versus a task you dread.

EXERCISE:

Which social networks are you currently posting on?

_____

_____

If you're overwhelmed by being a "jack-of-all-trades," which social networks will you let take a backseat for now? Remember, you can go back to it later.

_____

_____

_____

_____

_____

CHAPTER 13

Overcoming Writer's Block: What to Blog About When You Don't Know What to Blog About

"A blog is a perfect way to keep your talkers fed with new topics and ideas. Everything you post gives people something new to talk about."

— Andy Sernovitz

In the last three chapters, you have read about increasing your visibility with social media, tapping into the lead-generating power of LinkedIn (the world's largest network for business professionals) and how to eliminate feeling overwhelmed by social media marketing.

Many people don't realize it, but blogging is not only cost-effective; it's one of the most valuable social media marketing tools in their marketing toolbox. To me, blogging is the core of social media. Why? Because when you post a blog on your website, you can then go out on social networks and tell your followers about it—provide a link that takes them to your blog and generates traffic to your site.

FIVE BENEFITS OF BLOGGING

Blogging is a great way to convey your expertise without pitching prospects. They read your posts—which should be informational and entertaining in nature—and learn more about who you are and what you have to offer.

It is not about hard core sales; it's about providing your readers with value. Sure, once in awhile you can say, "By the way, I'm offering this new product or service" with a "success story" that goes along with it. But blogging is about building credibility and, again, engaging and developing lasting relationships.

Five benefits of blogs are that they:

1. Are easy to use.
2. Help improve your website ranking.
3. Offer a way for you to share your expertise and knowledge with a larger audience.
4. Are a great way to build your list.
5. Are just as easy to update as your website (if not easier).

In an interview with blogging authority Michelle Shaeffer, I asked whether she attributed her success to her blog.

Her reply was, "Definitely, at this point it's what attracts a lot of traffic to my website. I can put up a website that just says, "Here are my products and services," but nobody wants to read about that. I have over a thousand articles on my blog—articles that are helpful guides and tutorials to different things."

"As a result, I get a lot of traffic to my site because when you can solve a problem for somebody and they see that, they realize that you've got some answers and then, they want to know more about you. My clients now come from my blog. It's really the main—and most cost-effective—marketing tool I use."

Having transitioned her business from website design to blogging trainer, Michelle believes that solopreneurs and business owners should "absolutely be blogging."

One reason is because creating a successful blog forces you to stop, focus on and answer these questions:

- Who are your ideal clients?
- What are their biggest problems that you can solve?
- What results do they need?

When you figure that out, you'll know what to write about in your blog. "It makes such a difference in your whole business," Michelle explained.

A great way to get people to comment is to join a blogging challenge or a blogging community. There is the Ultimate Blog Challenge, founded by Michelle and her colleague, Michele Scism, and now hosted by Paul Taubman and Danni Ackerman. You can find it at www.ultimateblogchallenge.com. It takes place every few months, but people continue to post after the challenge is over as well.

There are also groups on Facebook designed to gather like-minded people together and comment on one another's blogs.

EIGHT IDEAS TO GET YOUR CREATIVE JUICES FLOWING

At the beginning of each new year, it seems, from Facebook to Twitter, many people start writing about their goals or asking what others have planned for the coming year. One year, I found myself faced with writer's block, wondering what to write about. So I thought, "Why not write about what to write about?"

Whether you are posting blogs on your website, tips on your Facebook fan page, or writing a newsletter, coming up with fresh content on a consistent basis can be a challenge.

Here are eight helpful ideas to charge your batteries and get your creative juices flowing. Take note of the ones that resonate with you, and by the time you are done reading, I hope you'll have a great list to get you started.

1. Success stories. Do you have a product or service (old or new) that generates great results for your customers? Share them with others. Don't be afraid to ask your customers for feedback on their experiences as well. Then, write about them and let others know the good news.

2. "How to" features. Most people like knowing they're going to get a finite set of tips, guidelines or secrets. With this in mind, you can write about "Ten Smart Ways to Lose Weight Without Even Trying," "Twelve Pointers for Writing Killer Headlines," "Four Ways to Get Great Results from Your Realtor," etc.

3. Company information. Choose stories that acknowledge your achievements and lend credibility to your business. Customers/prospects read about how others respect you and, therefore, begin to look at you as an expert in your field.

4. People stories. People like reading about people—especially if it's someone whom they know personally. It could be about someone who did something outstanding to help your community—an employee who excelled in his/her role or a customer who received an honor or won an award.

5. Related interest stories. Is there something happening in current events that relates to your business (i.e., the economy, sustainability, solar energy, recycling, etc.)? Write about that.

6. Frequently asked questions. You see them on many websites. Why not compile a list of those questions you receive from customers or prospects? You may find you have enough to write about for a while. As you read on, you'll see that's what Michelle Shaeffer did.

7. Glossary. Are there words within your industry that need some explanation? While they may be commonplace terms to you, perhaps your audience members need some clarification before they really grasp their meanings.

8. Journaling. As you may have discovered, some folks simply write about what's going in their lives. I've seen posts about weight loss and fitness training written by Internet marketing professionals and business coaches. For instance, when *New York Times* best-selling author Joel Comm decided to shed some unwanted pounds, he posted about his weight loss and his fans followed him. They didn't say, "Why is he posting about this?" Instead, they felt closer to him and supported his journey every step along the way.

When my beautiful golden retriever, Ike, passed away, I wrote a blog post about it. Titled, "Fear Not Facebook," I explained how I found comfort from those who shared their heartfelt thoughts over the loss of my loyal four-legged companion.

The world of social media has made it possible for us to share more of ourselves on a daily basis and readers are responding positively to this. They like getting to know you on a more personal level. It helps you strengthen that know, like and trust factor.

BUILDING YOUR AUDIENCE WITH BLOGGING: AN ALTERNATIVE TO WRITING YOUR OWN CONTENT

Aside from attracting clients, learning how to blog—the right way—is really powerful. It transforms how you are able to connect with potential clients, understand them, and be able to offer your products and services to them.

Michelle suggests that, "Long term, blogging is the way to really build an audience. It is something that, once you have figured out how to get your content, not just on your own site, but on other sites (where your audience is), gets you noticed. You gain some credibility and your authority builds up quickly when guest blogging in combination with your own blog."

Michelle brings up a valid point. She and I have both guest blogged on each other's sites and I've reciprocated with other colleagues as well. Two benefits of these reciprocal blogging partnerships include:

- When you have writer's block, having a colleague contribute a guest blog helps you stay consistent with your posts without having to create new content.

■ When you're a guest on a colleague's blog and vice versa, you get viewed by "new pairs of eyes" from one another's audiences—helping one another generate traffic to both of your sites.

When I am a guest on a colleague's blog, I use social media marketing to get the message out and send traffic to the person's site. The colleague does the same for me when he or she is a guest on my blog. I even provide the person with a set of guidelines to consider when he or she is going to be a guest on my blog. You could do the same. Guest blogging is a great way to joint venture with a partner. (See more about joint ventures in Chapter 9.)

ARE YOU MARKETING ON YOUR OWN TERMS?

Blogging is like most things in business—those things that work the best take time, fine-tuning and figuring out. It has worked amazingly well for Michelle in her business.

"I enjoy writing so it's a natural fit for me. I also tend to be a night owl, so I work crazy hours. I can't pick up the phone and make cold calls at 3:00 a.m., but I can write a blog post at 3:00 a.m., schedule it with technology (see the reference to Hootsuite in Chapter 12) to publish at a specific time, and make that work for me.

"It's something that's given me a lot of flexibility and freedom to be able to do marketing on my own terms and my own time, my own schedule, what works for me. So I really like it for that reason."

ARE YOU SPEAKING YOUR PROSPECTS' LANGUAGE?: A THREE-STEP STRATEGY TO CREATE A FOLLOWING

You might be thinking, "I'm new to blogging. How do I create a following?"

Great question.

When Michelle started her blog, she started getting traffic from search engines and really didn't know why. "It's funny because having done website design for a long time, I understood keywords. However, I didn't do keyword research. I didn't look this up in Google, AdWords, AdSense, Word Tracker or any of these tools and people were finding me."

What Michelle realized was that traffic was being generated because she was *answering clients' questions in their language*. She naturally used the phrases that they used, so people from the search engines were finding her that way.

Because the strategy Michelle used was answering her clients' needs, that's where her traffic started coming from.

Keep this three-step strategy in mind:

1. Look at the questions your clients are asking you.
2. Write down their questions (in the language they used to ask it).
3. Answer their questions.

If you don't like doing keyword research, this strategy may work well for you. What worked well for Michelle was to focus on what the problems were in her clients' eyes as well as how they phrased them.

She would use those phrases in her blog post (i.e., talking about it in a way that they would talk about or type it into a search engine query). "So when Google changes their algorithm for the five zillionth time and everyone freaks out, my website traffic doesn't go down. It stays consistent because I'm not trying to gain search engines and I'm not overly optimizing. It's just natural."

FOUR MORE BLOGGING STRATEGIES FOR GAINING EXPOSURE

In Chapter 2, we talked about the importance of knowing your target market, ideal client and tribe. As you've turned the pages, I'm sure you've come to realize how this applies to all phases of your marketing. Blogging is no different.

Strategy #1: Taking time to understand your audience.

This was another strategy that worked well for Michelle (and can work for you). Ask yourself, "Whom did I write this for?" Then, send that person an email with the link and say, "Hey, you remember that question you asked me the other day? I just wrote a blog post about it. Here you go. If you find this helpful, would you share it?" When Michelle followed this strategy, she found that people started sharing her blog posts with their friends.

She explained that she would then sit down and brainstorm about, "Who else can I send this to?" I would send it to colleagues and say, "I wrote this blog post I think your audience would really love; would you mind tweeting it for me?"

"I took the time to write those emails and send them out, reaching out to people one-on-one. I did a lot of leg work like that. It wasn't just put the blog post up and traffic shows up. And when I share or tell someone some of the things I put on my blog, people respond with "Really? You do this?" My response is, "Yes, because it works," Michelle shared.

Strategy #2: In addition, as mentioned earlier, guest blogging is a great way to build relationships.

Even though she wasn't comfortable reaching out to people, Michelle found this was a good strategy to strengthen relationships with people who would repeatedly publish her content.

Therefore, she looked for sites that did column type blog posts—where every couple of weeks they would have another post from the same person. Then, she nurtured relationships with those people so she knew that every two weeks her guest post was going to go out to their audience.

"This allowed me to keep some consistent content going out. I didn't have to constantly go through the pitch process of saying, 'Hey, here's who I am; you should publish my stuff.'

"I asked myself, 'How can I do this?' And then I worked on finding strategies that allowed me to work within my comfort zone," continued Michelle.

Marketing can often take us outside our comfort zone. However, it is not a bad thing to start out by saying, "Well, if I'm going to do this, I should at least start out with things I'm comfortable with."

Both Michelle and I have written a lot of guest blog posts for friends or colleagues who didn't have a ton of traffic, but they had some traffic, and it was comprised of our ideal audiences, so it was worth pursuing.

How about you? Why not give this strategy some thought and gain exposure for your business?

Strategy #3: We also found that inviting others to post to our blogs was a great strategy because then they would promote it to their peeps.

As we talked about earlier, it introduces your readers—even if it's only to a few people—to someone who could help them. And it allows you to reach new audiences.

When I first met Michelle, I invited her to be a guest on my blog. She had a few posts on her site that I knew would resonate with my readers, and she was generous in sharing her tips over on my blog (and I reciprocated on hers as well).

Strategy #4: Writing reviews.

When Michelle bought a product or service she really liked, she'd write a review about it and then send the blog post link to the person who produced that product or service. Because it was a positive review, the person wanted to share it, and as a result, that person's audience would find her blog.

Another colleague of mine, Internet marketer Bonnie Gean, does this quite often with excellent results.

Consider these four strategies as well as thinking about how you can get someone else to share a post for you—someone who has an audience that fits your ideal client profile.

PUT YOUR HEART INTO IT AND GET OUT THERE

I think you'll agree that guest blogging is a very cost-effective way to get your message out there on a broader scale. It doesn't cost you any money to reach out to someone and say, "Would you share a blog with me, or can I share a blog with you?" or "I reviewed your product and posted a blog about it so wouldn't you like to share it with your peeps?"

Michelle explained that "Like a lot of people who are going to read your book, Debra, I had more time than money, and when you've got more time than money, in that phase of your business, that's what you've got to do—just get out there, put your heart into it and find what works. Just keep trying."

EXERCISE:

What are you going to blog about next? Do a little brainstorming and write down your ideas here.

_____

_____

_____

_____

_____

Have you bought any new products or used a new service you really liked? Write them down. Then, head on over to your blog and write a review.

_____

_____

_____

_____

_____

Whom would you like to contact within your network about being a guest on your blog?

_____

_____

_____

Which of your colleagues has a similar target audience, so it would make sense for you to be a guest on his or her blog?

_____

_____

_____

_____

_____

_____

CHAPTER 14

Finding Prospects from the Comfort of Your Home—In Your Pajamas or Sweats (And It's Not Social Media)

"Most people have 'one way' brains—they acquire information and do nothing. Guerillas have 'two way' brains—they obtain relevant information and act on it."

— Jay Conrad Levinson

In the previous pages, we have covered a lot about social media. However, there is a way to find clients from the comfort of your home—in your PJs or sweats. There are days that solo- and entrepreneurs don't want to get all dressed up and go out. And as your own boss, you have the freedom to make that decision and stay put.

So what is it, other than social media, that you can do from home in order to find your ideal clients?

SCAN AND READ BUSINESS AND TRADE PUBLICATIONS

Magazines and journals exist for almost any field you can think of. Local publications, national, and even international ones are out there depending on the industry you're involved with.

Are you reading them?

I hope so because if you're not, you are missing out on capturing potential leads and connections you can foster.

Read the appropriate publications—ones where you think your ideal clients are hanging out. Maybe you're interested in relationships, marketing, business coaching, environmental issues, animal rights, life coaching . . . . There are so many of them out there. I hope you're getting the picture.

While you are learning and gathering details from informative articles, there is something else I want you to pay careful attention to . . .

Take note of those people who have recently been promoted or have started a new business—people who are likely to be your prospects and ideal clients.

"I read a lot of the major publications for my particular industry and they're always downloaded on my Kindle," explained blogging authority Michelle Shaeffer. "And, in the past I have recommended to people that they go look for those opportunities to get themselves into those publications. I told someone the other day, 'You need to be in *Reason* magazine because it reaches the audience you're looking for,' but I never thought to do that the other way around and look for my own clients there. So this is a great tip because you'll be able to find those prospects on social media once you know who you're looking for."

For example, when I started out as a direct response copywriter, I read publications like *Direct*, *DM News*, *Inside Direct Mail*, *The Kauaʻi Business Report*, *Pacific Business Journal*, *The Denver Business Journal*, *ADWEEK*, and *Catalog Age*.

Then, when reading all these publications, in the articles and in the "People" sections, I would look for prospects. When I started my business, I focused on marketing, communications or creative directors because, at that time, that was the audience I was targeting.

For instance, if you are a technical writer, you would probably pay attention to personnel at high-tech companies. If you're a graphic designer or a photographer, you might pay attention to art and/or creative directors. What you will find is that, over time, you have collected quite an array of names. You might say, "Now what do I do with these names?"

As Michelle Shaeffer mentioned earlier, I suggest that you go online and take advantage of social networking. Do *not* start selling these people. Simply go to your favorite social network(s)—whether it's Facebook, Google Plus, Twitter or LinkedIn—interact with them and start building relationships with them.

As mentioned in Chapter 11, when you are on LinkedIn, take time to personalize your invitation to connect. Reinforce something from the article that you read about the person and mention it in your invite. Take a look at which groups people are participating in and join the conversation. I'm not talking about stalking here. Be genuine in your approach.

Brian Kurtz, Executive Vice President of Boardroom, Inc., said this, "I create time in my schedule to go through each one [LinkedIn requests], look at the profile, find an area or two of common interest or a group of people we share, and then I write a personal email acknowledging those synergies to make sure I can get some Vitamin C [Vitamin Connect, a term coined by Ned Hallowell that is mentioned in the next chapter] even while I am . . . yes . . . screen sucking."

You can "Like" someone's Fan Page and request to be his or her friend on Facebook, but along with that friend request, send a brief private message (PM). NOTE: Your private message may land in the "other" folder of the person's Facebook account, but it is still a good idea to take that extra step to reiterate how you met and why you're reaching out to connect with him or her. Most of the time, I have received replies to my PMs, and then a conversation begins.

Once you have that online engagement, follow up offline. Take a moment to send a note in the mail. Just a simple card that says, "Hi, how are you? Just wanted to say have a great day (and add something personal that the person may have posted on FB, Twitter or LinkedIn)."

"You really have to put something special (and personal) into ALL your communications," said Brian. "And if you start with what you can contribute to the other person first, it *always* works in terms of getting the maximum amount of Vitamin 'C' [connect] in your bloodstream."

When I first started my business, there was no email or social media marketing. Back then, I sent out a personalized letter to each person I had on my list of prospects. In addition to my phone number, I also included a postage-paid reply card to make it easy for people to respond.

So there you go. This is one tip you can do at home, with your laptop on your lap, in your bed, wearing your pajamas or your sweats—whatever you're most comfortable in. Just go and start reading, scanning trade and business publications and keep your eye out on the people who might be ideal prospects for you.

EXERCISE:

What publications (local, business, trade, etc.) are you reading?

_____

_____

_____

_____

_____

Pick up one of those publications and make a list of names that you can reach out to.

_____

_____

_____

_____

_____

CHAPTER 15

Gathering Your Tribe: Using Email to Build Your List

"An individual artist needs only a thousand true fans in her tribe. It's enough."

— Seth Godin

Tribe . . . fans . . . followers . . . . Whatever you call your "peeps," a crucial component of your marketing success is developing a community—people who turn to you because they value your expertise and knowledge. In the last chapter, we talked about building part of that community from the comfort of your home office—scanning trade and business publications.

Another way to gather your tribe is to provide them with information that makes their (personal and/or professional) lives easier. Once they arrive at your website, in addition to blog posts, you want to deliver something of value—something irresistible that encourages them to give you their names and email addresses.

As mentioned in Chapter 10, while you may have a large social media following, those names do not belong to you. Should any of the networks go away (remember MySpace?), those names go with them.

In her weekly e-newsletter called "The Social Scoop," Mari Smith referred to social networks as "rented land." She wrote, "Your blog should form the core of your overall content strategy in your business. This is your own 'land.' Whereas, your social channels are all 'rented' land. Yes, it's important to build a loyal audience on your preferred social sites (Facebook and Twitter recommended, at minimum), but also provide regular invitations to come read your blog, join your email list and, of course, ultimately do business with you!"

Laura Rubinstein, author of *Social Media Myths Busted* and co-founder of Social Buzz Club, put it this way, "Suppose you've accumulated 50,000 connections between your top three networks, and one day your best, most engaged network changes its rules or determines you've violated their terms . . . . They could remove your connections because of some algorithm change or, worse yet, they could close your account and never let you have access again with no good reason."

Ms. Rubinstein goes on to explain a situation where she was shut down on LinkedIn, so she speaks from personal experience. She said, "Here's the good news, if you've already started growing your connections on the social networks: This audience is now *primed* for you to bring them 'home' to your website, add them to your email and blog lists, and introduce to them other opportunities and offerings on your site and in-person."

Internet marketer and author of *Trust Funnel*, Brian G. Johnson, found success in connecting with people on social networks and sharing marketing content with them from his blog on those networks. "It really pulled it together for me. It allowed me to get traffic by standing out and being unique, being authentic and having a brand. That is what resonated with people—not all the people, but that's okay . . . . You can't really satisfy everybody."

MOTIVATING YOUR AUDIENCE

According to The Radicati Group's Email Statistics Report 2013-2017, the total number of email accounts is expected to grow to 4.9 billion by the end of 2017 (up from 3.9 billion in 2013). Back in October 2001, International Data Corp. projected that the number of email addresses would grow from 505 million to 1.2 billion email boxes. We've come a long way, baby, haven't we?

When you are engaging with your community and people get to your website, how do you motivate them to opt in (i.e., give you their email addresses) so that you can continue to engage with them and build on that relationship?

Russell Kern, founder of KERN, an Omnicom Agency, offers suggestions on fundamental strategies that motivate your audience to respond to your message (whether you're doing consumer or business-to-business marketing). He suggests that your offer meet three criteria:

1. It must be unique, capturing emotions or filling a person's need.
2. It must be exclusive. If you are the single source of a given offer, it drives action.
3. It must be valuable, offering time savings, money savings and/ or emotional relief. Or in business-to-business, it must offer access to information that fuels success, competition or insight.

Direct marketer Bob Hacker, founder of The Hacker Group, says,

"Use fear to motivate your target audience to pay attention to your mailings. Tell prospects about the 15 ways they can get fired from their job, and then promise a white paper that tells them 15 ways they can prevent termination."

I suggest that you use love (or another positive emotion). For instance, a variation on Bob's recommendation might be, "Fifteen ways you can find a fabulous job that fuels your passion and pays the bills."

EMAIL: ARE YOU USING IT OR ABUSING IT?

In his book *Write Everything Right*, Denny Hatch reported that according to *Fortune/CNN*, the average person receives 147 emails a day and deletes nearly 50 percent of them.

When it comes to email, are you using it or abusing it? Here are several guidelines to remember when implementing your email campaign.

Guideline #1. Get permission from your customers/prospects.

Email to customers and willing recipients tied for first place with affiliate programs as the most effective choice for building website traffic, according to a study conducted by Cambridge-based Forrester Research. The key word to pay attention to here is "willing." If you're going to conduct an email campaign, be sure the people you are sending your message to have "opted-in" (i.e., they have asked to receive email about products or services like yours).

Email service provider MailChimp sends billions of emails a month for its customers. It reiterates the importance of permission and says, "If your initial reaction . . . was, 'But what if . . . ,' then stop what you're doing, because you most likely don't have permission.

"Permission means that people requested email marketing from you. Before investing your time and money in an email-marketing program, start getting permission from your customers. It's easier than you think, and it'll result in fewer spam complaints, better deliverability, decreased legal liability, and—most importantly—better open and click results."

Industry statistics reported by *DM News* show that consumers who opted in bought five to seven times more frequently than those who visited a site anonymously.

Guideline #2. Don't overdo your emails.

A visit to VerticalResponse's website says, "'How often should I email?' We get this question all the time, should it be twice per month, twice per week, once per quarter? The truth is that we don't have a perfect answer to this question. What we do know is that it all depends on the relationship you've built with your recipients.

"Over-mailing your recipients is a very effective way to lose subscribers! A bored or annoyed recipient is one step away from becoming an unsubscribe and you really don't want to alienate your subscribers.

"Under-mailing your recipients can be as equally dangerous, especially if you've spent a lot of time and money to convert new leads to newsletter subscribers. Don't wait too long before sending an initial welcome email because you want your recipients to get familiar with your content and your static 'From Label' right away."

Author of *Amazon's Dirty Little Secrets*, Greg Jameson says, "Believe it or not, if you don't send enough emails, people will stop thinking about you and/or think you don't have anything useful to provide. I've gotten up to three emails a day from some companies, which I find annoying—in fact one email a week might even be annoying to some. But one email a week is certainly not intrusive, and if you only send one email a month, you are likely not maximizing your email marketing."

When I first started implementing email as part of my marketing strategy, I was sending out an e-newsletter once every quarter! It was in one of my online marketing groups that a colleague said, "Hey, Debra, I think you better step it up or your peeps may forget who you are."

I not only switched to a monthly e-newsletter, but I signed up for an email service (I use Aweber) and began communicating with my community on a more consistent basis.

When asked how often he emails his list, Brian G. Johnson said, "One of the nice things about being an entrepreneur is you get to decide what's right for you. Some people will mail their list three offers a day. That's great, that's not wrong, that's not right, that's what they do. Some people will mail their list once a week. Same thing, not wrong or right, it's just what they do.

"For me, I do keep in contact regularly so people remember and think, 'Hey, it's that Brian guy again.' And, hopefully, they're thinking nice thoughts.

"One of the things I talk about when discussing the mailing list subject is that you're basically creating two experiences for people when you email them. Chances are you're annoying or you are providing value. There are going to be some people that are kind of in the middle and they could care less and hit the delete button. So, I'm always trying to add value and email people on a fairly regular basis.

"I don't go looking for a product to sell. I don't try to find something to make me money, but when I find something I'm really excited about, I'm going to tell my subscribers about it. I'm going to push it hard and not feel bad about selling to my list because they signed up and asked for information from me—information to help them move forward in their marketing. If I feel really positive about a product in particular, then why shouldn't I feel good about promoting it to them?

"If I don't have something to sell, I might send people to a blog post with a video about mindsets. So, it becomes a really powerful circle of synergy. . . . I'm always trying to add value to my list."

In other words, send your customers a message only when you have something of value to share with them. As Brian Johnson mentioned, it might be a product you strongly believe in—one you know will help their business grow and prosper. Or it might be a reference to a blog post or video where nothing is being sold; you're just offering beneficial and insightful tips, pointers or guidelines for whatever industry you're in. I know my subscribers like getting information about writing copy, where to get images for their blog posts, tools for video creation and the like.

Guideline #3. Give careful thought to the content of your messages.

Start with a compelling or personal subject line. Your subject line is like the teaser on the outer envelope of a direct mail package. If it is not meaningful, it isn't opened. Make sure it doesn't sound like spam or they will hit that delete button faster than you can say the word.

In Chapter 18, you'll read, "Do Your Headlines Go Ka-Ching?" When I presented this topic at a virtual conference for *Direct Marketing IQ*, a couple of attendees asked whether these tips apply to subject lines. The answer is, "Yes."

The big difference in email subject lines is, of course, length— you only have about fifty characters. Here are six quick tips for writing email subject lines that reiterate the pointers that you will find in Chapter 18.

Tip 1. Offer a benefit. Customers buy for one of two reasons: To gain something they do not have or to avoid losing something they already have. With that in mind, how will the content of your email lead them toward satisfying a burning desire or help them avoid losing something they already possess?

For example, "Three tips for staying motivated when times get tough." or "The secret to writing rock-solid headlines."

Tip 2. Offer news. Use words such as "announcing," "introducing," or "now available for the first time . . . ." One subject line I wrote read: "Some interesting YouTube stats." It had a 48 percent open rate. According to MailChimp, the average open rate for my industry (i.e., marketing and advertising)—for campaigns that went to at least one thousand subscribers—was 18.81 percent.

Tip 3. Ask a question. Pique their curiosity. For instance, "Are you feeling like a winner today?" or "What makes you special?"

"Is your marketing content generating great leads?" is a subject line I used in one of my auto responders and it received a 32 percent open rate.

Tip 4. Create a sense of urgency. As you would in a call-to-action, give prospects a reason to take action quickly (i.e., a time-limited savings, contest deadline, etc.).

A colleague of mine was offering a savings on his annual membership site. He did a series of messages from "Tic-tock, less than seven hours to go" to "Get it now, coupon expires at midnight."

Tip 5. Use social proof. Have others taken the action you want your prospects to take? I received an email from Facebook authority Amy Porterfield about a program she was launching with the subject line "Are you like these people?" In the message, she mentioned that hundreds of people had already signed up—she was using social proof to encourage action.

Tip 6. Be real. Offer something that shows you are human. People relate to people. For instance, once when I presented a webinar, I was three-quarters of the way through the program before I realized the audience couldn't hear me. I sent out an email saying, "Was my face red." I explained what had happened and how embarrassed I was. It had a 70 percent open rate! I was "human." People appreciate integrity and honesty.

Guideline #4: Like all direct marketing promotions (yes, email is direct marketing), talk to your customers in a friendly conversational tone.

Remind recipients that they are getting this message because they gave you permission. For instance, you might start with, "You're receiving this message because you signed up for our list," or "....because you agreed you wanted to receive updates from us."

Personalize your message. When you're using auto-responders (such as Aweber, MailChimp, Get Response, etc.), it is easy to program the recipient's first name into your message. Like direct mail, a personalized message saying "Dear Mary" works better than "Dear Friend." Therefore, insert the customer's first name in the greeting.

Greg Jameson reiterates this point in his book: "People like getting emails that are addressed to them, not 'Dear Customer.' They also appreciate getting emails that are from someone, not a company. Sign your name to your emails!"

Get to the point. Keep it simple. Make it easy for viewers to determine what you are offering them. Give them benefits and do not forget a call-to-action. Do you want them to reply with a "Yes" to your email, click through to your URL, or sign up for an event? Tell them what you want them to do.

Guideline #5: Choose your time wisely.

Everyone is busy. Pick the time of day to send messages wisely. The middle of the day is a good time because people often have many messages to sift through first thing in the morning. Avoid Monday morning; try Wednesdays around 12:30 p.m. instead. You may want to avoid Fridays as that is a day people seem anxious to leave the office and start their weekend.

Guideline #6: Respond to your customers' inquiries and questions.

Respond to your customers within twenty-four hours. Remember, marketing is about building relationships. Please do not ignore responses from customers. Use every opportunity to engage with them.

If someone unsubscribes from your list, you need to accommodate that request. At first, you might think "Shoot, I lost him." But, trust me, it is okay. You don't want people on your list if they don't want to be there. In some cases, they may be doing you a favor because you don't need someone subscribing to your list if he isn't even going to open your messages. However, if you are so inclined, you can send a quick message thanking him for having been a subscriber and suggest that, should he ever change his mind, you would be happy to hear from him.

I had one person unsubscribe from my list, but after a few emails back and forth, she changed her mind. She appreciated my reaching out and that shifted her thinking about the value she received from my messages.

"Your list is your bank account, but if you build it on service and relationships, it will be your retirement account."

— Patty Farmer

EXERCISE:

What are you currently doing to build a community?

_____

_____

_____

_____

_____

What is your irresistible offer to encourage people to opt-in?

_____

_____

_____

_____

What information can you share that your subscribers will be
"hungry" for and excited to receive?

_____

_____

_____

_____

Can you repurpose something you have done in the past and convert it into a free report, a video training series, an eBook? Write down your ideas here:

_____

_____

_____

_____

_____

_____

CHAPTER 16

Are You Talking to Me? The Importance of Word-of-Mouth Marketing

"If you build a great experience, customers tell each other about that. Word of mouth is very powerful."

— Jeff Bezos

Did you know that 90 percent of consumers trust peer recommendations over advertising? (Only 14 percent say they trust advertisers.) It's my guess that you may not find the statistic all that surprising. After all, if you think about it, when you need a new dentist or doctor, chances are you won't turn to the Yellow Pages or Google and search for one. You—most likely—will call upon a friend, relative or trusted colleague and ask for a referral.

When you're seeking a recommendation from friends, you turn to them because you want to find a service provider they know, like and trust.

In his book *Word of Mouth Marketing*, Andy Sernovitz wrote, "People will ask other people about you before they decide to buy from you. We turn to people we trust first . . . Not ads, not brochures, not phone books."

"It's [word of mouth marketing] about real people and why those real people would want to talk about you and your stuff . . . . I've been marketing for a long time, but I've never had a marketing budget. Despite that, I've sold a lot of stuff. Any success I've had has always been half creativity and half talking to a lot of people."

It's no wonder that 82 percent of small businesses say that word-of-mouth (WOM) is still the main source where new customers find out about them. The reliance on word-of-mouth marketing has led many small businesses to make social media marketing one of the leading tools in their marketing toolbox.

People write reviews from anywhere from Amazon and eBay to TripAdvisor and Yelp. It has never been easier for your customers to share their opinions and spread the word about their experiences.

However, word-of-mouth has been around long before social media marketing came on the scene. There's certainly Facebook, but don't forget face-to-face. That's right—the good old tradition of offline social networking—meeting people in person!

Author Ned Hallowell said, "You are the master of what this world needs most . . . the power of connection. I call it the other Vitamin C, Vitamin Connect, and we live in a world where most people suffer from a deficiency of it.

"Glued to their electronics, they get massive doses of electronic connection, which in no way imparts the life-enhancing, indeed life-saving power of the true Vitamin Connect. For [true connection] you need face to face, human connection. SO much comes across in what I call the human moment," continued Hallowell.

Before the Internet age, business people relied on getting out of the office to professional meetings to network, greet fellow colleagues and build relationships. Socially, we went out to dinner or to parties and looked each other in the eyes instead of down at our tablets or smartphones.

Building relationships—that's what it's all about. And today, more than ever before, it's important to "meet & greet," shake hands and have a personal conversation with clients and prospects—not just one that's typed in an email or text message.

That is where a lot of WOM begins. "Millions of people blog, millions more post online reviews, and everyone Googles you," wrote Andy. "But even more is happening offline—as it always has. Each and every one of us talks to a friend or family member before we buy something . . . . And we don't just ask for advice—we also make recommendations about what we liked and what we hated."

In an article published in *Pacific Business News*, a Waikiki entrepreneur was quoted as saying "hundreds of professionals [are] making time for midweek business networking events in Hawai'i, a scene that has taken off . . . .

"People are starting to realize, especially in this economy, that you have to get out, put your face out there, build your credibility so you can not only grow your own business, but help others with new contacts."

Don't forget to put yourself out there in public among potential prospects who will appreciate meeting you in person and enjoy having the opportunity to shake your hand and laugh together out loud instead of "LOL" online. It can lead to valuable referrals, resources, friendships and a steady stream of happy, new clients.

CREATING THAT BUZZ ABOUT YOUR BIZ

You may be out there networking (read Chapter 2) and discovering that people are beginning to talk about you in a positive way. If you are online typing away on Facebook, Twitter, LinkedIn or whatever your social network of choice is, good for you. Social networking certainly should not be ignored.

However, you may be thinking, "How do I convey that buzz online—get others talking about my business (or me)? How do I convert prospects into loyal raving fans?"

CONVEYING PROOF—SOCIAL PROOF

One of the best ways to tell the story about your product or service is to demonstrate the benefits—show people that what you promise is what you deliver. When prospects know other people have used your product and read about the results, they're more likely to click on that "buy now" button and make a purchase.

In my opinion, one reason why Amazon continues to be successful is it asks customers to post reviews about their purchases. Those reviews help convert prospects into new customers.

In an interview, Joel Comm said, "I find getting other outlets to speak about you—free publicity—creating a story that is compelling so that the story is told about you by others, has been the most profitable payoff for me.

"If I can create a story around one of my products, services or a stunt that I do and I can get Tech Crunch, Mashable or some bloggers to write about it, that's going to drive traffic and interest."

As both Joel and Michelle Shaeffer suggested (in Chapter 13), many bloggers write reviews on their blogs. They review products, books, online training programs, hotels and more.

Andy Sernovitz writes, "How can a single blogger with her list of gripes and raves have more impact than *Time* or *Newsweek*? It's because the person is part of a community—a community that seeks out information about things its members care about and shares those opinions through word of mouth."

Show how your product or service solves your prospects' problems and makes their lives easier.

FIVE WAYS YOU CAN DEMONSTRATE SOCIAL PROOF ONLINE AND START THE WORD-OF-MOUTH FLOWING

#1. Testimonials—the power of praise

I strongly believe in the power of praise that comes from your customers and satisfied clients—past and present. As ad man David Ogilvy said, "If you include a testimonial in your copy, you make it more credible. Readers find the endorsements of fellow consumers more persuasive than the puffery of anonymous copywriters."

What types of testimonials should you use? Ones that illustrate how your customers successfully put your product/service to work for them. You want more than "It was good" or "I loved it." Look for feedback that communicates results such as "Your service increased my income by xx dollars," "Your product helped me lose xx number of pounds in just two weeks," or "I got rid of my back pain in xx number of days."

For instance, a client of mine emailed me saying I had done a great job, but here's how she said it: "The text on my landing page felt clumsy and out of focus, and I wasn't seeing the results I wanted with conversion rates. Debra waved her magic wand and in just a few simple, laser-focused steps, guided me in making my text much stronger and clearer for my ideal clients to more easily 'get it' and connect with my message. She has a way of boiling things down so that you take away powerful, easy-to-apply tools and tips, without feeling any overwhelm."

Much more revealing than "Debra did a great job," don't you agree?

How do you get testimonials? Just ask.

Most customers are happy to give them, yet they may not think to share their thoughts without a request from you. When they do provide their feedback, ask for their permission before you post it publicly. If they're hesitant about your using their name, ask whether you can use their first initial and last name, first name and last initial or just their initials along with a city and state.

If you'd like a template that I use to request testimonials from satisfied customers, email me and I'll send it your way. For more details on how clients can praise your services, visit this post on my blog at www.writedirection.com/testimonial-approach/

#2. Case studies—showing before & after results

These are similar to testimonials, but more detailed. A case study shows where a person or business was before the purchase, how he or she used the product, how long the results took, and what the results were.

People like the specifics, and the "before and after" story paints a picture they can relate to. I'm sure you've seen this strategy used a lot with beauty, weight loss and fitness products.

#3. Videos—take prospects on a tour or share customers' thoughts

Don't just tell prospects about your product, but take them on an inside peek with video. A video demonstration of how to use your product shows prospects exactly what to expect.

Give viewers ten tips or five pointers that catch their attention and create desire. If your product is an e-book, you can show them the Table of Contents and a page here and there. You can also highlight and talk about any bonuses you may be offering.

Better yet, ask your customers to submit testimonials on video. A colleague of mine was doing a demo of his product at a local health food store. Later that day, he told me how, after tasting it, one of the customers raved about his product. My first reply? "Did you get it on video?"

He had not, but since then, he has taken my tip to heart. Now when he's doing a demo, anytime someone compliments his product, he pulls out his smartphone and asks for permission to record the person's feedback. Then he uploads it to YouTube, his Facebook profile and his website. There you go—word-of-mouth straight from a happy customer reaching a broader audience in just a few minutes.

According to YouTube, over six billion hours of video are watched each month on its platform—that's almost an hour for every person on Earth. With Internet viewers spending this much time watching videos, it is a great cost-effective marketing tool—growing by leaps and bounds. There is a reason YouTube has become the third most visited website and the second largest search engine (as of this writing).

#4. Flash your credentials

Are you a published author, an expert in your field for more than ten years, or someone quoted in a newspaper or interviewed by other experts in your industry? Let people know. Write about it on your blog, your website's "About" page, and put it in your email signature.

These credentials help you build credibility and paint a picture of you as an authority on your subject.

#5. Free trial period

Sometimes you can get the "tire-kickers" to buy if you get them behind the wheel for a test drive. If it makes sense for your product/service, consider offering a fourteen or thirty-day free trial and encourage prospects to try out what you have to offer.

Touch base with them during the trial period to see how they're doing and answer their questions. Deliver good customer service, and at the end of the trial period, a happy prospect may become your next loyal, paying customer. A loyal customer will have good things to say about you to his or her friends, family and colleagues, and the resulting word-of-mouth begins paving a trail to your door.

TWO LITTLE WORDS THAT HAVE A BIG IMPACT

When customers take the time to praise you, don't forget to thank them! I can't stress this enough. This is vital if you want to continue that steady stream of optimism oozing from your happy fans. They are promoting your product/service/program for you . . . supporting your business . . . increasing your exposure, for free.

Do not take that for granted. "They deserve a little thanks—and, conveniently, thanks is all they want in return for their hard work. They feel like part of the family," wrote Andy Sernovitz.

It doesn't take much to show you're grateful for their enthusiasm. Anytime I receive a comment on my blog, a "thumbs up" on Facebook or LinkedIn, a retweet on Twitter, or a +1 on Google Plus, I always respond with a "Thank you."

When someone has taken the time to write a testimonial or share positive feedback, you can be sure that person receives my gratitude. After a subscriber commented on my blog, I sent out an email express-ing my appreciation. She responded by complimenting me for always sending a note of thanks each time she posted a comment, and she suggested I write a blog post about it. I did—it was a great idea. (You never know where your inspiration will come from.)

In addition, I am still someone who takes a pen in hand, writes a "thank you" note and puts it in the mail. I can't emphasize the impor-tance of letting your fans know that you appreciate them. I do this, not only with clients, but with colleagues who send me client referrals or connect me with other professionals to collaborate with.

WORD-OF-MOUTH IS WHERE IT'S AT

Nielsen's Global Trust in Advertising survey revealed that 92 per-cent of consumers (around the world) say they trust earned media such as word-of-mouth and recommendations from friends and family, above all other forms of advertising.

Many of the strategies mentioned in this book are successful ways for getting your name out there among customers and prospects—creating top-of-mind awareness. Over time, you may find that when the phone rings, the person on the other end has never met you, but someone else has and has passed along your name. And, to me, the referral network aka word-of-mouth is the most cost-effective advertising there is.

"If the only prayer you ever say in your entire life is thank you, it will be enough."

— Meister Eckhart

EXERCISE:

How can you build social proof? Do something for others. List two ideas you can post on your blog that provide valuable information to your prospects.

1. _____

2. _____

Write down the names of four people you can contact to request testimonials:

1. _____

2. _____

3. _____

4. _____

Who are the "talkers" in your community—people who can help you spread the word?

_____

Do you have any before & after case studies you can use? What are they?

_____

_____

_____

_____

Make a list of people you are going to write thank you notes to today:

_____

_____

_____

_____

CHAPTER 17

Awakening the Copywriter within You

"Do the stuff only you can do. One thing you have that no one else has is YOU—your voice, your mind, your story, your vision."

— Neil Gaiman

Throughout each chapter, you have been reading about business-building strategies designed to help you get exposure, expand your connections, and create a flow of loyal, raving fans so that you drive revenue to, rather than deplete, your bank account.

If I am correct, you want to help others, and I wrote this book because I want to help you in making your business more successful. In this chapter, I want to awaken the copywriter within you so that when someone clicks on your website (or reads any type of marketing material, for that matter), that person resonates with your message. He or she will then gladly read your content instead of moving on and clicking onto a competitor's site.

As creative, heart- and soul-centered entrepreneurs and business owners, one of the most important tools we have in offering our programs and services is the copy we use to communicate our messages. So the question arises: How do you best express your passion to your audience in a way that reaches out and get results?

There is one magic bullet for communicating your passion, attracting more clients and making a difference in their lives. That bullet is *copy*—or the words you use to express your message. After all, you can't have marketing materials—whether it's a brochure, direct mail letter or a Web sales page—without the words, can you?

Mark Twain wrote, "The difference between the right word and almost the right word, is the difference between "lightning" and "lightning bug." And little has changed since he wrote that.

Marketing mentor Adam Urbanski says, "The right word in the right place spells success . . . to thrive in this world, you simply must command a well-rounded vocabulary. Like it or not, the world responds to words."

So you can see the importance of creating captivating content—it is really vital.

KISS YOUR PROSPECTS

When you want to write compelling copy that is easy for your prospects and customers to read . . . KISS them!

While some people equate this acronym with "Keep it simple, stupid," I prefer to use "Keep it simple, sweetheart."

Clarity is extremely important in writing marketing content—be it a brochure, blog, direct mail piece or website. As Herschell Gordon Lewis said in *The Art of Writing Copy*, "Clarity has to come first, no matter what you're writing or to whom."

Dr. Flint McGlaughin puts it this way, "Clarity trumps persuasion."

You want to create a conversation between you and your audience, but how do you do that when you're not face-to-face?

One way is to imagine you are sitting across the table from your ideal client and having a conversation. Or you can do the visualization I described in Chapter 3. Then, when you sit down to write, keep this in mind . . .

The difference between conversation and writing is that during a conversation, you give the other person time to understand what you've said. You pause between sentences, repeat yourself and space your ideas apart.

The secret of writing is to leave space—create these pauses—on paper (or on the Internet).

I encourage you to go to Amazon and pick up a copy of *The Art of Plain Talk* by Rudolf Flesch. (I got my copy from my mentor Eugene Schwartz back in 1988—it was first published in the '60s as *In the Art of Plain Talk*). In that book, he outlined these seven steps that will really help you make your writing inviting:

1. Use short, simple sentences to start out with—average sentence length in words:

8 words or less is considered very easy
11 words – easy
14 words – fairly easy
17 words – standard (Average Reader)
21 words – fairly difficult

25 words – difficult

29+ words – very difficult

2. Two short sentences are easier to read than one long one. In direct marketing the rules of grammar may not always apply. (For example, sometimes copywriters use one word sentences. Break long sentences into shorter ones.) It does depend on your market—if they're highly educated (i.e., lawyers, educators, etc.), they may be seeking language that is grammatically correct.

I admire what copywriter Herschell Gordon Lewis advises about grammar: "Copywriters are communicators, not grammarians. What matters isn't your knowledge of which tense is which; it's your knowledge of how to transform the lead of drab fact into the gold of lustrous attraction."

2a. One additional piece of advice I often give when reviewing content (and I know you've heard it before—not just from me), is to use bullet points. When there's a lengthy paragraph, rather than make your audience plow through that, break it up into easy to read bullet points. Make the content inviting to the readers' eyes.

3. Be personal. Use the word "you." "You" is one of the strongest words in the marketing lexicon.

You're writing to a reader—one who is a current customer or prospect—so talk to that reader. Avoid mentioning "the client" or "the customer." Let your prospect know you're talking directly to him or her, one-on-one. Use the word "you."

The readers come first—start writing to people (not at them). Incorporate a friendly, conversational tone as if your reader were sitting right there—across the table from you.

In his book, *Direct mail copy that sells!*, Herschell Gordon Lewis explained, "When you write a letter that says, 'Only you . . .', you've told the recipient that to you he isn't a unit, an anonymous number in a computer, a faceless organism with a zip code . . . You also project an attitude of friendliness."

4. Whenever possible, talk about people. Tests show that we enjoy, and are better readers when, reading about other people more than about anything else. Sentences can be written so that the logical subject is a person. Use personal pronouns (you, yours, theirs) or human interest words (woman, man, child, girl, boy).

David Ogilvy said you can strengthen your headline by adding emotional words such as darling, love, fear, proud, friend and baby.

5. Use active verb forms that have life in them (i.e., dance, sing, add, run, etc.). These words make your sentences "move." Here are some examples:

> **Passive:** The stadium was the site of a rally led by
> CU's Buff Boosters today.
> **Active:** CU's Buff Boosters led a highly-spirited rally
> at the stadium today.

> **Passive:** The basement was flooded with water.
> **Active:** Water flooded the basement. Or better yet—Water
> rushed rapidly through the windows, flooding the basement.

> **Passive:** The door was opened by Joe.
> **Active:** Joe opened the door. Or better yet—Joe kicked
> open the door!

6. Punctuation makes reading easier. It gets pauses down on paper and stresses important points. Use hyphens, dashes, and ellipses to achieve this effect.

7. Give the reader helpful advice or service. This tip comes from ad man David Ogilvy, who said, "It hooks about 75% more readers than copy which deals entirely with the product."

So, are you KISSing your readers?

WRITING FROM THE CORE OF YOUR BEING

In the last few years, I have seen a shift happening in the world of online marketing. I am guessing you've seen it too. It's a shift from content that hypes a product (or makes claims that can't be substantiated) to a heart-centered approach that resonates with people in a kinder, gentler way.

"Marketing and writing with heart, not hype" has been my tag line because it is a philosophy I've valued for a long time.

I even stepped down from a project once when my client asked me to make promises that his product was not going to deliver. An important tip to remember, is "Don't make promises you can't keep" because bad news travels fast (faster than good). You want that positive word-of-mouth—not negative reviews—spreading like wildfire.

INSIGHTFUL GUIDELINES FROM DR. SEUSS

So how do you write from the core of your being and communicate a message that speaks to your audience's desires?

With the help of a great philosopher—Dr. Seuss—here are three guidelines to follow:

1. Come from your heart. After all, what matters is what's in your heart and who you are as a person. Share your message from a caring place. Be genuine in your message.

> *"Be who you are and say what you feel because those who mind don't matter and those who matter don't mind."*

> — Dr. Seuss

I have a client who said to me, "'Be authentic' is beginning to sound so cliché." And, as a result, he was hesitant to say what he really wanted to share with others because he wasn't sure his message was different.

When we continued to talk, his enthusiasm for his work and how he approached his style of coaching was different—it was unique to him, and I encouraged him to keep that in mind and go with that as he moved forward.

I believe that you can't go wrong when you are authentic and speak your truth. Keep in mind what I've said earlier: people want to work with those people who have the KLT Factor—people who show compassion and concern for the issues they face daily.

"People buy from people they like. When you allow your personality to come through, people feel a sense of intimacy with you. They begin to trust you. And like you. Rapport is built. And sales happen . . . . People want to read words from a trusted friend," wrote Joe Vitale, author of *Hypnotic Writing*.

2. Think about your product, program or service and start from that place deep inside you that really wants to help others. You know you're good at what you do, so own your brilliance, share it, and let your radiant light shine.

"Today you are you, that is truer than true.
There is no one alive who is youer than you."

— Dr. Seuss

As you write, feel what you are trying to convey—let some emotions seep in. After all, when you're telling a story face-to-face when talking to a friend, you move your hands, change your inflection, move your eyes, your body, and more.

As Joe Vitale said, "Put excitement into your writing. Let go. Feel emotion. Get moved and you'll move your reader . . . write . . . with all the spontaneous energy and enthusiasm you have. Be yourself. Don't write to impress; write to share a feeling."

Right now, I want you to focus on what you want to attract into your business. I want you to play along with me here and take a moment, close your eyes, take a few deep breaths and visualize this.

I want you to see yourself in the office or workspace you desire, having clients come to you who fit your ideal client profile. Envision them leaving with smiles on their faces, grateful for your help, and you are grateful because you're experiencing the joy and satisfaction you deserve. What does that look like to you?

When you are done visualizing, grab a pen and paper and start writing the vision that came to you.

3. Be confident about who you are, what you have to offer and how you help people.

"Why fit in when you were born to stand out?"

— Dr. Seuss

Your attitude and your visible confidence are two qualities that attract people to you. When you're confident about yourself—as well as the program or service you're offering and how it helps your ideal clients—that clarity comes across in your marketing message and people respond to it in a positive way.

ARE YOU WRITING FROM THE CORE OF YOUR BEING?

When teaching an online course about copywriting, I received an email from one of the group's participants. She asked, "How can I tap into my writing ability?" I said, "You awaken the copywriter within." Let me explain . . .

Every morning, I listen to a guided meditation from Deepak Chopra. Every few months, he co-hosts a 21-Day Meditation Challenge with Oprah Winfrey. If you've never participated in one of these challenges, I highly recommend it.

One of the meditations was about the "Miraculous You." And one day while I listened, this idea for a blog post came to me. Yes, thoughts do pop up constantly while I'm meditating, and after many years at it, I finally learned that it's not about quieting the mind, but just allowing it to be.

After finishing my meditation, I began to write. In response to

"How do you awaken the copywriter within you?" I decided the answer was fairly simple.

BE YOURSELF

In my humble opinion, life is about relationships (and so is marketing), but first, there is the relationship with one's self.

Be genuine and realize it is okay for the world to see who you truly are. I think some of the most engaging and inviting content I've seen comes from heartfelt professionals who are okay with being transparent.

Being transparent helps your prospects and customers feel closer to you—an essential step in boosting sales with trust and integrity.

My client I mentioned earlier (the vocal coach who was concerned that authenticity was cliché) doesn't consider himself a marketer or copywriter. But what he does is bring his sincerity and honesty to the table.

Deepak Chopra said, "If you've been caught up in an anxious search for love, happiness or anything else, you can let go of the struggle and endless quest for self-improvement. And, instead, begin to open to the awareness of who you really are."

And I like what my colleague Cindy Schulson says; she puts it this way, "Learn from others, but trust yourself. Trust yourself to make the right decisions and that you know what you're here to do. Embrace who you are and let that show up in your business in a real way."

Who are you? As I explained earlier, speak from your heart. You can share:

1. Your own challenges.
2. How you overcame them.
3. How you can now help others (who are in
   similar situations) succeed.

When you do this, you relate to people and people relate back to you, so they develop a stronger bond with you because of your common experience.

For instance, I started my business in 1989 after looking for a J-O-B. Colorado was in a recession at the time, and everywhere I went, prospective employers said, "We're not hiring; we're laying people off." I was frustrated and, needless to say, worried because I had a mortgage to pay.

However, those people who said they weren't hiring also said, "Debra, if you were a freelancer, we could use your services." Hence, The Write Direction was born. And as a result, when I share this story with others who wish to be in business for themselves, they're encouraged by it—especially since I'm still standing twenty-five-plus years later.

I'm going to suggest that you sit down with a pen and paper (this stimulates your subconscious more than typing on a keyboard) and just write.

Joe Vitale says he commands or requests the writing from his unconscious, and he explains that "Some of the greatest writers of all time did not THINK through their writing. Instead, they listened to something within and just wrote."

My mentor, Gene Schwartz, would set a timer and write in 33:33 minute spurts.

I write Morning Pages each morning—three pages of stream-of-consciousness writing.

I've read that direct response copywriter Dan Kennedy writes for an hour each morning, no matter what. The point is that these writers keep the door open to their unconscious—allowing creativity to come on in.

Joe Vitale writes, "…my first big secret is that when I sit to write, I do it without much of an idea of what I will say."

As you read this book, you're gathering the tools you need to stand out and shine in a way that is natural and true to who you are. Don't worry about what comes out; just be real and put your thoughts down on paper. Let it flow—uncensored, without judging yourself.

You can fine tune it later, or if you are really struggling, consider handing it off to a copywriter to assist you with fine-tuning it so it flows after you have written a first draft.

PERFECTIONISTS! GO EASY ON YOURSELF

"Have no fear of perfection, you'll never achieve it." — Salvador Dali

"I have learned a fundamental key to success: Don't wait for perfection . . . . Don't let striving for perfection stand in the way of getting results." — Joe Vitale

"Sloppy success is better than perfect mediocrity."
— Alex Mandossian

"The essence of being human is that one does not seek perfection."
— George Orwell

"Practice means what it says: writing is something to be done over and over, something that improves through the repetitive doing but that needs not be done perfectly . . . Consistency is the key to mastering the instrument that is you." — Julia Cameron

"No good work whatever can be perfect, and the demand for perfection is always a sign of a misunderstanding of the ends of art." — John Ruskin

These quotes are just food for thought when you feel like you are banging your head against a wall and seeking perfection.

As we have explored in this chapter (and coming up in the next), there are certainly guidelines to follow for writing captivating content that converts your prospects into customers.

However, a good beginning—even if you hire a copywriter to write for you—is to look inside yourself. Who is the person you want to be? Let your personality shine through because people want to know the real you, not a carbon copy of someone else.

Afraid of copywriting because you think you don't know what to say? Be yourself and awaken the copywriter within you. Or as Oscar Wilde said:

"Be yourself; everyone else is already taken."

I am always surprised how people will spend thousands of dollars on website design, yet don't get help with their content. A nice logo and pretty colors alone won't sell (unless maybe you're a photographer or artist)—you need magnetic words. Your words are what encourage, motivate and inspire prospects to take action.

Remember this: People want what you have to offer them. They want to transform their lives and you can help. You can make a difference. I know you can.

Now is the time to let your light shine!

EXERCISE:

Pick up a pen and paper now. What's the first thing that comes to mind after reading this chapter? Don't give it a second thought; just write it down now.

_____

_____

_____

_____

What are the personality traits people use to describe you?

_____

_____

_____

_____

How do you describe yourself?

_____

_____

_____

_____

Are you sharing your authentic self with your audience?
If not, what's holding you back?

_____

_____

_____

_____

What challenges have you had in your life?
How did you overcome them?

_____

_____

_____

_____

CHAPTER 18

Do Your Headlines Go Ka-Ching?

*"What sells—what motivates people
to take action—are words."*

— Joe Vitale

Now that you're on the path to awakening the copywriter within you, this chapter reveals some tips to help you hone your skills. After all, you can't have marketing materials—whether it's a direct mail package, video sales letter or a website—without the words, can you?

When you are writing copy, you have a scant one to three seconds to catch a prospect's attention online and approximately five seconds if you are sending out a direct mail piece. Therefore, your goal is to catch his or her attention long enough for your prospect to decide to continue reading all of your content.

In Chapter 3, I mentioned my mentor, Eugene Schwartz, who was a veteran direct response copywriter admired by many in the industry. In his book *Breakthrough Advertising*, he wrote, "your headline has only one job—to stop your prospect and compel him or her to read the second sentence of your ad." As advertising guru David Ogilvy said,

"On the average, 5 times as many people read the headlines as read the body copy."

TWELVE POINTERS FOR CREATING A ROCK-SOLID HEADLINE THAT GRABS ATTENTION

1. Ask a question in the headline. "With 1 in 2 people getting osteoarthritis in their lifetime, can you afford to ignore your joints?"

A classic headline used for a promotion for *Psychology Today* was "Do you close the bathroom door even when you're the only one home?"

What's one question that comes to mind for you? Write it down now.

2. Give news using words such as "introducing," "announcing," "now available," or "new." "Announcing ten remarkable ways to stay in shape without exercising daily," or "Now available, a new report reveals three ways to find lasting love after you've kissed your ex goodbye."

3. Address your prospects' concerns. This type of headline helps you push your prospects' buttons so that, while they're reading, they are thinking, "Yes, I need/want this. I gotta have it." For instance, in 2008 and '09, people had real concerns about the value of their real estate so this addressed their concerns:

"Facing foreclosure? Here are three questions to ask your lender before they take your home away from you," or "Need money now? Here are ten legitimate ways to make a quick buck."

4. Promise something wonderful, but do not lie. You'll lose more customers than you gain that way. (Bad news travels fast.) Plus, in this day and age, being honest is top of mind. It builds trust, and people respect you when you're genuine.

For instance, the headline just mentioned "Ten legitimate ways to make a quick buck" better deliver ten ways—sincere and honest ways—that prospects can take advantage of.

Marketing strategist Jim Connolly put it this way, "Using sensational headlines, to get people to open emails or read content, is a super-fast way to lose the trust and respect of your marketplace." I agree with him; don't you?

5. Be specific. This well-known Rolls Royce headline from David Ogilvy did the job: "At 60 miles an hour, the loudest noise in this new Rolls Royce comes from the electric clock."

6. Give the reader a command—tell him/her to do something. "Go ahead, throw away this *free* offer."

7. Promise your prospects helpful/useful information. "Five reasons why using numbers in your headlines work," or "Four tips for losing weight without feeling starved for your favorite foods."

8. Promise to reveal a secret. "Discover the secret to writing thought-provoking, compelling copy," or "Explore the secret to connecting and engaging with your prospects." NOTE: Be sure you do indeed reveal the secret. I've said it before and will say it again, bad news travels faster than good when you disappoint your customers.

9. Give your prospects good news. "You're never too old to tone your body and be in great shape," or "How to attract the love of your life without compromising your values."

10. Target a particular type of reader. "Do you aspire to write children's books?"

11. Tie in to current events. The most well-known example of this is the "Official car (camera, airline, beverage, etc.) of the Olympics."

12. Highlight your guarantee. "Lose ten pounds in ten days or your money back."

In *Breakthrough Advertising*, Eugene Schwartz also wrote, "They (headlines) are the invitation to your ad—the hand you extend to your prospect for your product." As a bonus, since I've mentioned Gene several times throughout this book, here are six of his favorite tips for writing great headlines:

1. State the claim as a question. "Could you use $200 a week extra income?" or "Who else wants a whiter wash—with no hard work?"

2. State the difference in your headline. "The difference in premium gasoline is right in the additives." (I know when I'm at the gas station, there's always a sign on top of the pump about how its gas is better than others.)

3. Address the people who can't buy your product. "If you've already taken your annual vacation, don't read this. It will break your heart."

4. Address your prospect directly. "To the man (or woman) who will settle for nothing less than the presidency of his firm."

5. Accuse the claim of being too good. "Is it immoral to make money this easily?"

6. Challenge the prospect's present limiting beliefs. "You are twice as smart as you think."

MAGNETIC WORDS YOU CAN USE

At last	Guaranteed	Revealing
Exciting	How-to	Time-sensitive
Exclusive	Love	Urgent
Fantastic	Limited offer	Breakthrough
Free	Powerful	Special

Some words ad man David Ogilvy adds to this list (from *Confessions of an Advertising Man*) are:

New	Amazing	Easy
Suddenly	Sensational	Wanted
It's here	Revolutionary	The truth about
Just arrived	Miracle	Bargain
Improvement	Magic	Last chance

THE SECRET TO WRITING GREAT COPY

The secret to writing great copy is that it is all about people!

For instance, a woman or man considering a weight loss program isn't buying the program—they are buying what the program does for them. It may help them regain their self-confidence . . . stop feeling insecure if their husband/wife looks at another woman/man . . . bring back love and sensuality into their life . . . feel attractive again to their partner . . . eliminate their frustration over yo-yo diets that have them keeping a closet full of skinny vs. fat clothes, etc.

It is about the woman or man, their feelings and emotions—not the program they're buying. Get the picture? I hope so.

When writing copy, it is important to do what I call "pushing your prospects' buttons." As I mentioned in Chapter 3, you may hear some marketers call this "tapping into your prospects' pain." Either way, it is about determining their problems, reaching out and touching people's emotions in a way that shows you understand and have a solution that will help them.

For example, when asked, "What's your biggest challenge?" many entrepreneurs and business owners say, "I need more clients." However, what does that mean? What is the impact or spillover effect of not having enough clients?

When probing further, the deeper issues of how this challenge impacts other areas of their lives are revealed. Without new clients, they are not making enough money to pay their bills. Because they're not earning enough income, they are stressed out about debt and don't sleep well at night. They have problems at home with their spouses so their relationships are suffering, their children feel ignored and are not performing well in school, they are discouraged and depressed and the list goes on and on.

In Chapter 3, we talked about understanding your ideal clients and the problems that keep them awake at night. When your marketing copy demonstrates that you understand the cost of their pain and how it affects their career, health, family, finances and priorities, your prospects resonate with your message and want what you have to offer. When their buttons are pushed, they have an "aha" moment that results in taking action—that action is one where they turn to you for help in relieving their pain.

ONE OF THE BEST WAYS TO IMPROVE YOUR SKILLS

In copywriting, as with so many other skills, one of the best ways to improve your own abilities is to study the greats—learn from others (like I learned from Gene Schwartz).

Marketers and copywriters of all levels keep what are known as "swipe files"—files of great headlines and other copy that worked for someone else—to study and rely on for inspiration.

Contrary to the name, these aren't meant to be copied directly, but rather used as jumping off points for your own creative brilliance.

Using swipe files can improve your own headlines almost immediately. Mentally run your topic through a few of the examples in any given list and you're practically guaranteed to come up with a winning headline backed by some serious testing historical clout.

Of course, you'll get better and better at writing headlines the more you practice. Try out several headlines for every piece you write instead of just going with the first one that comes to mind.

Hundreds—if not thousands—of headline swipe files are available online; a quick Google search will show you that. Here are a few online resources that you'll find extremely helpful:

- Who's Mailing What—the Ultimate Swipe File —www.whosmailingwhat.com/
- Copyblogger's free eBook, "How to Write Magnetic Headlines."
- Jon Morrow's "52 Headline Hacks: A Cheat Sheet for Writing Blog Posts that Go Viral."

- And my own "Twelve Pointers for Writing Attention-Getting Headlines and A Baker's Dozen of Fill-in-the-Blank Templates You Can Use Right Away."

THREE TIPS FOR CREATING YOUR OWN SWIPE FILE

In addition to the resources I mentioned above, your own swipe file could be a:

1. Document on your computer where you can copy and paste irresistible headlines you find online.

2. Folder in your email program where you tuck away emails with headlines that compelled you to open them.

3. File for those direct mail pieces you received in your mail box (yes, good ol' "snail mail") that grabbed your attention.

Finding the styles that speak to you, in these swipe files and elsewhere, helps you develop your skill with writing headlines that get read—and better yet—*acted upon.*

Below, you'll find some fill-in-the-blank templates you can experiment with. But before you do, I thought it would be worthwhile to share some *before* and *after* headlines with you as well. Take a look and see which one you find more appealing. Which one(s) is boring vs. brilliant or mediocre vs. monetizing?

Before: A woman's guide to finding true love

After: How to Attract the Love of Your Life Without Compromising Your Values (it may be longer, but it's simple and speaks to the results)

Before: Grow your business with social media

After: With 10 Minutes a Day and Access to the Internet, You Can Tap Into Endless Business Opportunities Using These Proven Social Marketing Strategies

Before: Turn your passion into money in the bank

After: Transform Your Passion and Expertise into a Profit-Generating Empire with This Six-Step Money-Making Webinar System

Before: Five steps to get a promotion

After: The Introvert's Guide to Getting Noticed and Promoted at Work

A dental practice was starting an educational program to help dental assistants improve their skills and get the training they needed to be Registered Dental Assistants (and earn more money). They sent me a flyer that said:

Before: Who we are (on one side) and What we do (on the other)

After: Want to be more than an employee working in a dental office? Increase your value—and your earnings up to 60%—as a Registered Dental Assistant

> *"Long headlines that say something are more effective than short headlines that say nothing."*
>
> — John Caples

EXERCISE:

It's your turn to take a stab at it. Here are five templates (along with examples). Take some time, brainstorm and fill in the blanks as they apply to you, your business and your target market.

- Introducing 5 tips to _____without _____.

  Example: "Introducing 5 tips to shed those pounds without giving up the foods you love."

- With _____ can you afford to/not to_____?

  Example: "With almost 1 billion users on Facebook, can you afford not to have a Fan Page for your business?" or "With 1 in 2 people getting osteoarthritis in their lifetime, can you afford to ignore your joints?"

- 10 things your _____ won't tell you about _____, even if you asked.

  Example: "10 things your doctor won't tell you about weight loss, even if you asked. After all, if you knew them, you just might lose weight."

- 3 secrets _____ don't want you to know about.

  Example: "3 little secrets your boyfriend doesn't want you to know about and how to get him to let you in on them."

- 5 biggest mistakes _____ make and how to avoid them.

  Example: "5 biggest mistakes investors make and how to avoid them."

CHAPTER 19

Giving Up Is Not an Option—Eight Secrets for Succeeding in Business

"And the day came when the risk to remain tight in a bud was more painful that the risk it took to blossom."

— Anaïs Nin

Having started my business in 1989, running my business as a solopreneur, I discovered eight secrets that really helped me along my journey to success.

To tell you the truth, I didn't really know these secrets when I started, but as I look back, I realize that they are guidelines that have served me well—and will serve you well as you move forward with your business.

SECRET #1: BELIEVE IN YOURSELF

When I first started my business and people asked me, "Are you good at what you do?" I didn't hesitate with an answer, I said, "Yes" right away. I actually surprised myself when I did that. I wasn't being cocky or arrogant, I was confident.

Why else would I be going out on my own if I didn't feel I had something to offer others? I will admit, it helped that my mentors boosted my confidence level. I was lucky to have two of them, both seasoned veterans in the field of copywriting. They were very encouraging about the talent they saw in me, and that motivated me.

Remind yourself that you are good at what you do—good at helping people, making them feel really comfortable, or helping them move past feeling overwhelmed.

Get clear and then excited about doing what you do. When you feel yourself wavering, turn to your mentor, your coach, or a trusted colleague for support and that person will remind you of the gift that you have to offer and your brilliance. So keep that in mind. Secret #1 is "Believe in yourself."

SECRET #2: BE GRATEFUL EVERY DAY—*EVERY DAY*

Daily gratitude changes your vibration. I'd like to share an excerpt from Dr. Rick Hanson's book entitled, *Just One Thing: Developing a Buddha Brain One Simple Practice at a Time*. In a chapter about being grateful, he has this to say:

"Gratitude means paying attention to the offerings that have come your way—especially the little ones in everyday life.

"When you do this, you're resting your mind increasingly on good things moving toward you, on being supported, on feelings of fullness—on the sense of having an open heart that moves toward an open hand."

Dr. Hanson goes on to say, "Fuller and fuller, more and more fed by life instead of drained by it, you naturally feel like you have more of value inside yourself and more to offer to others."

I think that's beautiful; don't you agree?

Really quickly while you are reading this chapter, I want you to look around and notice what's around you—the gifts of birds singing nearby, flowers in bloom, perhaps a rainbow or waterfall, a child at play, a ray of sunshine. Then, I want you to be *grateful!*

Write below one thing you are grateful for today:

_____

Sometimes when we think about having a gratitude journal or stopping to think about what we're grateful for, we think, "It's gotta to be a really big thing like I landed an awesome contract today," or "I made a million dollars this year."

But it's really just the simple things like the sunshine and similar things that we can connect with on a daily basis. No matter what's going on in life, there is always something simple to be grateful for.

In one of his weekly emails, Brian Kurtz wrote, "As soon as I fall into 'there's too much on my plate' mode, I take a deep breath, think about all the things I am grateful for . . . and 'stressed' quickly becomes 'blessed.'"

Colleague Michelle Shaeffer interviewed me on this topic once; I turned to her and asked what she was grateful for that day. She said, "When I wake up, my commute to my office is about thirty seconds, my coffee pot is an arm's reach away. And when my children wake up,

I'm here and I can be with them and spend time with them and I've got the freedom to be able to do all of that because of this business I have. That's something I'm really grateful for."

It really helps me to focus on gratitude and to realize that no matter what else is going on, I have so much to be thankful for. To be honest, it took me a while to learn this lesson. I would do gratitude journals or just lay in bed in the morning or at night and sometimes I'd come up with the same stuff like "I'm grateful for the roof over my head." And I'd say to myself, "Well, you were grateful for that yesterday; there should be something new on your list today." But the truth was that I was still grateful for that roof over my head.

So remind yourself that it doesn't have to be "Oh I made a million dollars today." It can just be something as simple as noticing the vibrant color of flowers along your walk. You know that saying, "Don't forget to smell the roses?" It's simple and true.

SECRET #3: DON'T EXPECT OTHERS TO GET YOU RESULTS

You are responsible for your own results—for your own success. You can learn from other people's wisdom, you can follow their advice, but you have to take it on yourself and turn that advice into something that applies to you—then go out there and use it.

I like the way my colleague, international speaker Kevin Knebl, explains this. Think of it like this:

You go to a health club, thinking about joining and becoming a member. The club's personal trainer can show you the exercise machines, the weights, the pool, etc., but he can't turn you into Adonis—he can't lift the weights for you or swim the laps across the pool. I would love someone to lift the weights for me, but that's just not going to happen.

So remember this: You are responsible for your own success.

SECRET #4: BE YOURSELF. PEOPLE BUY YOU AS MUCH AS (IF NOT MORE THAN) YOUR SERVICES

We're all individuals with different needs, personalities, etc. If you buy into the concept that you're just a writer, just a designer, or just a photographer, etc., you won't be in business for as long as you like (or for twenty-five years, if that's what you desire).

Please keep these two thoughts in mind:

> *"Let the world know you as you are,*
> *not as you think you should be."*

— Fanny Brice

> *"To be yourself in a world that is constantly trying to make*
> *you something else is the greatest accomplishment."*

— Ralph Waldo Emerson

SECRET #5: GIVE YOURSELF PERMISSION TO DO WHAT YOU REALLY LOVE TO DO. IN OTHER WORDS, SAY "YES" TO YOURSELF

That's the benefit of being an enthusiastic and creative solopreneur—you do not have a boss, there is no one controlling you, no one is saying, "No." You're the only one who might say, "No" to yourself.

Do you find that you are saying, "No" to yourself a lot in your life?

I ask because, for the longest time I said, "No" to myself when it came to taking a break—just a short break—in the middle of the day. I said, "No, you have to work." I said, "No" to going to a dance or yoga class in the morning or midday for that matter because I "had" to work. Who said I had to? ME! Then, I finally gave myself permission—said, "Hey, Debra, you're the boss; you can do what you want."

And you know what? When you give yourself permission to nurture yourself—you also nurture your business.

It is interesting, isn't it? Interesting how we can be harder on ourselves than any boss we may have ever had on a J-O-B.

And that is why I am sharing these pointers with you—because I want you to learn from the mistakes I made. And I'm grateful that I have learned from them myself, but it did take some time.

Many of the things that it takes to build a successful business really are about having that confidence in yourself, being who you are and giving yourself permission to do what you love. And some of that is how you express yourself through business—by being good at the things you do. But some may be activities like yoga, dance or things that connect us to that love that we have for ourselves. It's easy to say, "No." I know because I have been my own worst boss too many times.

Step back and say, "Wait a minute; why do I have a business? Is it so I can work, like a crazy woman, twenty-four hours a day, or is it because I wanted to create freedom in my life, to do what I love, spend time with my family or my friends?" And if it is, then you should give yourself permission to do that.

It is important to be aware that you really are in charge of yourself. Don't let your business run you. You have got to be the CEO and run your business. Give yourself that time.

What I tell people (and I do this myself) is to put it down on your calendar. Schedule time with yourself just like you would schedule a phone call with a client. I do that now, I put my dance class on my calendar; there are times when I say, "Oh, a client needs me, so I better skip the dance class." But I don't do it all the time any more.

Having your own business is about having the freedom to do that. Sometimes you will put your business first, sometimes, but not all the time. You can also schedule time specifically to work on your business instead of in your business. When you put it on your calendar, it's so much easier to make sure you get it done.

SECRET #6: DON'T OVERTHINK THINGS

Don't look for a problem where there isn't one. Don't create one when one does not exist. I know I have a tendency to do this a lot—still today. Just writing this book, I had a tendency to get overwhelmed, thinking there is so much to do, feeling like there is not enough time to do it. Believe me; if you are like me, stop, breathe and learn just to take one step at a time. And ask for support when you need it.

SECRET #7: BE KIND TO YOURSELF

Nurture yourself; acknowledge your strengths. Remember your brilliance. When you finish reading this chapter, I want you to do the "Discover Your Brilliance" exercise. I have my clients do this, and it is an "AHA" moment for them when they realize just how much they have accomplished, but have forgotten about.

In this exercise, I'd like you to write down all that you've achieved since you started your business. For instance:

- Articles you have written (including guest blog posts).
- Awards you have won or acknowledgments you've received.
- Places you have been asked to speak (including webinars or teleseminars).
- Committees you have served on or volunteer work you've done.
- Interviews you've given for a publication, podcast or Blog Talk Radio show.
- *Whatever* you can think of that has made you feel good and let you shine!

During our interview, Michelle Shaeffer shared this, "Secret #7 really hit me because confidence is something that I have always had a lot of struggles with. And one of the key things I do now, at least once a week (though I try to do it daily), is to sit down and write out a list of the good things I accomplished—things I got done, sometimes they're small things, sometimes they're bigger things, doesn't matter; I have to write down what I got done. And when I can look back over that I go, 'You know what, I got some pretty cool stuff done regardless of what else is going on.'

"And it really does help to acknowledge yourself for those things you are doing right. We tend to get so focused on the future, on what we want to build, that we forget that we're doing really cool stuff today that we should celebrate and take a minute to say, 'Hey I accomplished something. I am good at what I do.' I love that!"

The first time I wrote my list, I surprised myself with how many pages I filled. Like me, I think you will also be pleasantly surprised.

Last but not least, one piece of advice I always give to people who call me or ask me questions about staying in business through the long haul is:

SECRET #8: BE CONSISTENT AND PERSISTENT. DON'T GIVE UP THE SHIP

For me, when I started my business back in 1989, giving up was not an option. About two and a half years into it, when times looked a bit shaky, I took a part-time job. At first, I was embarrassed, imagining people would see me working in a retail store and think I wasn't successful.

However, I quickly let go of that when I realized the reason I was doing it was to keep my business going. And here I am, more than twenty-five years later. To inspire you to keep on keeping on, I would like to share my favorite quote from Calvin Coolidge once again:

"Nothing in the world can take the place of persistence. Talent will not; nothing is more common than unsuccessful men with talent. Genius will not; unrewarded genius is almost a proverb. Education will not; the world is full of educated derelicts. Persistence and determination alone are omnipotent."

These eight secrets have seen me through more than a quarter of a century in business. I know they will see you through as you move forward with yours.

EXERCISE:

List five things you're grateful for.

1. _____

2. _____

3. _____

4. _____

5. _____

What are three things you achieved today
(perhaps reading this book is one of them)?

1. _____

2. _____

3. _____

What's one thing that is holding you back?
Is there someone you can turn to for support and/or assistance?

_____

_____

_____

_____

What are three things you can do to nurture yourself?

1. _____

2. _____

3. _____

Conquering Your Fears and Going for It

"Fear keeps us focused on the past or worried about the future. If we can acknowledge our fear, we can realize that right now we are okay."

— Thich Nhat Hanh

I think many of us started out with big dreams as children. Perhaps as a teenager, you had dreams and went into college ready to pursue them. Or were you still full of questions, trying to figure what you wanted to do with your life?

Like me, maybe you went to college, received a degree and then ended up on a path that wasn't quite what you anticipated. It can be more than a little bit scary to step back, stop and say, "This is not satisfying my needs. Now I am going to move in a different direction."

It took me getting physically ill to leave the field of speech pathology and find a new path. Maybe you found yourself without a job because you were working for a company that downsized or something drastic changed in your life. Then you were pushed into going for that dream and starting your own business because it seemed to be the best option at the time. That is I how ended up starting my business more than two decades ago.

Making a change and starting your own business definitely is frightening. But when you know there's something you can do to be in service to others, that you are meant to do or you just love doing, it is worth it to take that leap of faith and go for it.

I pursued a career as a copywriter with very little experience, but I had two things going for me: 1) two mentors and 2) a dream. That's right—a dream and a strong desire to pursue it.

I am fortunate that the encouragement I received from both of my mentors gave me the confidence to keep moving forward. My dream drove me to be consistent and persistent in my pursuit—and here it is more than twenty-five years later.

There have been ups and downs, days when I was in tears, but I stayed the course. I did not give up. As a result, I have had the good fortune of owning a business that allowed me to live in Boulder, Colorado, and on the magnificent Garden Island of Kaua`i, Hawaii. I consider myself lucky to have three places I call home (New York, Boulder and Kaua`i) and the ability to travel between them.

However, before I started to write this book, I once again found myself asking, "What do I want to be when I grow up?" I love writing, but it can be a lonely job—just me, myself, and my computer. So I started to re-evaluate my path . . . seeking my heart's message.

In doing so, I realized that, for years, my friends have said that I'm the "glue that holds them together." Jokingly, I would say, "If only I could bottle that and make it a business" because what I value is connection and community—building relationships.

Throughout this book, you have seen me mention the importance of building relationships. That's not only what marketing is about, but what life is about. I believe we all want to love and be loved, to nurture and be nurtured. We are all wired for relationships.

So once again I am making a shift in my business—one that continues to nurture relationships. And the funny thing is that it is related to my childhood dream of acting and being in the spotlight (you read about it in Chapter 5).

While I have delivered many presentations over the years—offline and online—I want to do even more. Speaking professionally puts me out there, connecting with others face-to-face, creating a community and serving its members by providing valuable information that helps them succeed.

Is this transition scary? Yes. Do I have days where I doubt myself? Yes. When I have these moments of fear, I have conversations with myself . . . journal about it . . . call on supportive colleagues. Then, I put one foot in front of the other and continue on. I want the same for you.

As a speaker, author, direct response copywriter and multi-faceted marketing mentor, I've pulled back the curtain and shared what has worked for me over the years.

I want to encourage and inspire you to create a lifestyle that provides you with the flexibility, fun and freedom to do what you love with people you love working with.

I believe it is time for each of us to let our lights shine and live our dreams. If you are afraid, know that you are not alone. Don't hold back. People want what *you* have to offer them. They want to transform their lives and you can help them. You *can* make a difference. I know you can.

Author and trainer Brendon Burchard said, "Becoming a great marketer is like anything else—you master it by learning from others, doing it yourself, experimenting, testing, and improving. . . . Your message deserves to be heard by the masses, and you deserve to make money when serving others."

Throughout these pages, it has been my goal to provide you with practical and creative tools to market yourself. Put one foot in front of the other and get your message out there so that you too can serve others in the best way you know how.

Now that I've shared my insights and strategies with you, I hope you will contact me and share your dreams and aspirations. Perhaps I can help you along your journey. Remember, you're not alone. Connect with others and build your relationship capital every step along the way.

It is not always easy, but when you follow your heart's calling, it is definitely worth the ride. I encourage you to take action today, as soon as you're done reading this book. Even if it is just one tip, implement it right away, while it is still fresh in your mind. Tomorrow, execute another tip and keep on going.

As my colleague Patrick Snow wrote in his book *Creating Your Own Destiny*, "Creating your own destiny is a life-long battle within your mind where you take action every day to fulfill your dreams. It is a battle you will win when you set your intention and continue on with persistence."

Let your mind be quiet and your heart lead the way. Conquer any fears you may have and go for it.

Here's to your sweet success,

Debra Jason

Debra Jason

About the Author

Debra Jason is an author, professional speaker, direct response copywriter, and multi-faceted marketing and copywriting mentor. A recipient of the Rocky Mountain Direct Marketing Association's (RMDMA) "Creative Person of the Year Award," she started The Write Direction in 1989. Since then, she has personally written thousands upon thousands of words for hundreds of clients around the country and overseas.

When other writers have researched books on direct response copywriting and freelancing, they have turned to Debra for her input. She has been quoted in such books as *Modern Media Writing*, *Smart Business Solutions: Direct Marketing & Customer Management*, *Copywriting Success* and more.

Debra is also a contributing author with *New York Times* best-selling author Joel Comm, of *So What Do You Do? Discovering the Genius Next Door with One Simple Question*. In addition, she has written articles for local, national and international trade and business publications such as *Direct, DMNews, Direct Marketing IQ, Direkt, Inside Direct Mail, iMarketing News, The Review, The Denver Business Journal, Kaua`i Business Report, Boulder County Business Report*, and *The Garden Island*.

Born and raised in New York City, Debra received her Master's degree at the University of Colorado at Boulder. Having lived on the island of Kaua`i, Hawai`i, for ten years, she calls these three places home as each one holds a piece of heart.

Currently residing in Boulder, Colorado, Debra treasures time with family and friends, loves dancing, yoga, the serenity of the ocean, and memories of walking her beautiful (and famous) golden retriever, Ike, along the white sand beaches of the incredible north shore of Kaua`i.

Copywriting and Marketing Coaching/Consulting

*M*arketing and writing with heart, not hype.

In 2012, after ten years living in paradise on Kaua`i, Hawai`i, Debra Jason returned to Boulder, Colorado where she first started her business, The Write Direction, as a freelance direct response copywriter.

With more than two decades of experience as a writer, speaker and marketer, she educates and inspires creative, heart- and soul-centered professionals to communicate their marketing messages in ways that captivate and convert their prospects into loyal, raving fans—*even* if they have been struggling with how to transform their ideas into words in the past.

Don't feel overwhelmed by the idea of writing your own content, marketing your business, or even starting your own business. Let Debra serve as your personal coach, consultant or mentor and guide you through the process so you move forward with ease and confidence.

She wants you to see what is possible and what you can create in your business. She serves as the bridge to get you there. Her mission is to empower you with cost-effective power tools and business-building strategies that you need to gain exposure for your business so that you attract a steady stream of happy clients while driving revenue to your bank account.

You are here to make a difference, and Debra is here to help you do that. When you get your message out into the world and serve others, you generate more income and can experience the joy-filled freedom lifestyle you've always dreamed about. After all, that's why you went into business for yourself to begin with. Isn't it?

For more information on how you can work with Debra or to sign up for a 30-60 minute complimentary copywriting or marketing consultation, visit **www.WriteDirection.com** or contact Debra at **Debra@WriteDirection.com**

Book Debra Jason to Speak at Your Next Event

When it comes to choosing a professional speaker for your next event, you will find no one more capable of captivating your audience or colleagues than Debra Jason.

Known as a connector who enjoys interacting with her audience, Debra speaks on the value of building relationships and the art of engaging as they apply to attracting clients, generating leads and networking both online and off. Her presentations incorporate her honesty, integrity and heartwarming style, which attendees have described as inspirational, enthusiastic, energetic and educational.

Since 1989, Debra has delivered marketing seminars and workshops privately for small businesses and trade organizations/associations as well as at the university level. She also created the first social media program offered through the Office of Continuing Education and Training at Kaua`i Community College.

Whether your audience is 12 or 12,000 in North America or abroad, Debra can deliver a customized message of motivation for your meeting, conference or company workshop. She understands that your audience members want not only to be inspired, but to receive practical, innovative business-building strategies that they can implement right away.

Debra's speaking philosophy is to entertain your audience members with passion, optimism and real-life examples that inspire them along the road to success. They walk away feeling confident, encouraged and empowered to pursue their dreams.

When you are looking for a memorable, dynamic and engaging speaker who leaves your audience wanting more, book Debra Jason. To see whether she is available for your next meeting, contact her and schedule a complimentary pre-event phone interview today.

www.DebraJason.com
Debra@DebraJason.com